FISHING WITH MY OLD GUY

Also by Paul Quarrington

Novels
The Service
The Home Game
The Life of Hope
King Leary
Whale Music
Civilization

Nonfiction
Hometown Heroes

PAUL QUARRINGTON

FISHING
WITH MY
OLD GUY

The Hilarious Quest for the

Biggest Speckled Trout in the World

KODANSHA INTERNATIONAL
New York · Tokyo · London

Kodansha America, Inc.
114 Fifth Avenue, New York, New York 10011, U.S.A.

Kodansha International Ltd.
17-14 Otowa 1-chome, Bunkyo-ku, Tokyo 112, Japan

Published in 1996 by Kodansha America, Inc.
by arrangement with Greystone Books, a division of
Douglas & McIntyre Ltd., Vancouver, Canada.

First published in 1995 by Greystone Books.

Library of Congress Cataloging-in-Publication Data

Quarrington, Paul.
    Fishing with my old guy : the hilarious quest for the biggest speckled
trout in the world / Paul Quarrington.
        p.   cm.
    ISBN 1-56836-155-6 (hardcover)
    1. Brook trout fishing—Québec (Province)—Broadback River—
Anecdotes.   2. Fly fishing—Anecdotes.   3. Quarrington, Paul.
4. Deval, Gordon, 1930–   .   I. Title.
SH689.3.Q37   1996
799.1´755—dc20   96-26640

Book design by Peter Cocking

Printed in the United States of America

96 97 98 99 00 Q/FF 10 9 8 7 6 5 4 3 2 1

"Brook Trout are like chamber music in an age filled with a deafening cacophony of amplified sound."

ERNEST SCHWIEBERT, *Trout*

HERE COMES ONE OF THE ODDER disclaimers you're likely to see, wherein the author is going to own up to a certain amount of lying. Curiously—as you shall discover as you read these pages—I did not lie when I might reasonably be expected to do so. There are no large whoppers here. Instead I have peppered the manuscript with half-truths and invention. I have played fast and loose with the great god Chronos. Nevertheless, like any fisherman, I am willing to swear up and down that all between these covers is true.

Also, I have throughout the book used only the first names of my companions, as though fearful of endangering their wonderful innocence. However, they are fine men and their identities should be known. Gary is Gary Benson and Paulo's last name is Conceicao. Gordon is Gordon Deval, author, angler and 1994 All-Round Senior Canadian Casting Champion.

PROLOGUE

IN 1960, A YOUNG SALESMAN for the Canada Needle and Fishing Tackle Company was leafing through a copy of *Field & Stream*. The magazine related the following story:

> *Once upon a time* [this is not *exactly* how the article proceeded, but very close in spirit] *there was a man who went to the extreme north of the Canadian province of Quebec to search for gold. He and his wife journeyed to the shores of Lac Assinica. One day the prospector asked his wife to catch a pickerel for supper. She dutifully walked over to the water's edge and fired in a plug. She found herself wrestling with some monstrous creature. The wife pulled it onto land and stared at it, bewildered. This was no* doré. *Her husband returned home and looked at the fish, equally stupified. It was some sort of* truite, *for sure, but what kind? It looked like a speckled trout, except they didn't grow that large.* Did they?

At just over eleven pounds, this was the second largest brook, or speckled, trout ever taken on angling tackle. And it was taken in a place where the fish wasn't even supposed to be.

The young salesman from the Canada Needle and Fishing Tackle Company determined that fact soon enough, because he fired off some inquiries to the Quebec government. The officials responded that in the area he was asking about, the watershed of the Broadback River, there were only *les dorés* and *les grands brochets*, great northern pike.

The young salesman began to formulate a plan. He was determined to get to Assinica, to have a look for himself, because if the *second* largest speckled trout was swimming around up there, eager to sacrifice itself for the supper table, it seemed logical that the largest brookie ever was awaiting an opportunity to leap into the record books. The fourteen-and-a-half-pound fish caught by a man known only as Dr. Cook had remained the world's champ for forty-odd years, and it was high time, or so the salesman thought, for this to change.

The salesman looked at maps. He could get to Chibougamau, he noted, and to the north he saw that there was water, plenty of water, and he conjectured that it must be somehow possible to canoe up to Lac Assinica, and from there perhaps to the Broadback River. He asked a fishing buddy if he were willing to accompany him on such an adventure. The buddy agreed, and the two set off in the high summer.

The salesman left behind a wife and four children. They were well provided for, he told himself. Not only was his job going well, he had recently made quite a little bit of money producing and marketing O'Fishol, an aerosol spray that covered one's bait with a foul scent. So the buddies drove all the way to Chibougamau, even though the road ended in St.-Félicien. From there they'd bounced along a rocky trail that snaked treacherously through the Laurentide Mountains. They arrived in Chibougamau and went to the little air base just outside town, to discuss the ways and means of getting into the heart of the land.

One thing they discovered soon enough: they could forget about the canoe. The maps they had been looking at were sort of rough drafts, simplified versions of the area. They saw now how the land was interlaced with rivers and creeks, studded with small lakes, how navigation would be nearly impossible. Not only that, the rivers on the map were slashed with altitude lines, indicating falls of consequence.

Fly us in, the salesman said.

We can't.

They were informed—which is to say, this is the information that was transmitted in halting English, received in faulty French—that they could only go in under one of two circumstances. The first was, they could try to secure prospectors' licences. As far as fishing went, they either had to go to one of the camps that had been built (such is the power of magazines like *Field & Stream*, there were now three camps servicing *les sports*) or else they had to secure the services of a private guide.

Okay, bien fine, said the salesman. *Where can I find a guide?*

You can't, they answered. *They all work for one of the camps.*

The salesman and his buddy retired to the tavern in Chibougamau and mulled over the problem. They mulled it over for five days, although every so often the salesman would run to the telephone and try to convince the Quebec government that he was anxious to look for gold. This was easier for them to understand than the story about the big trouts. The government still thought the area was troutless, anyway. It had, they liked to say, *les dorés* and *les grands brochets.*

The waiter in the tavern—whose smattering of English made him their ally and only friend in town—came in one day with good news. A guide from one of the camps had been fired. *How can we find him?* the salesman wondered.

You just sit here, answered the waiter. *Wait in the tavern. He'll find you.*

Later that afternoon, a tiny man came into the tavern, obviously on the brink of a royal drunk. The waiter nodded in his direction. The salesman and his buddy came up beside him, each taking an arm. The man was so insubstantial that they managed with no difficulty to lift him, his feet kicking semifrantically in the air, and thus they escorted him back to their table.

The man's name was Maxim Moisim. He was a good guide, everyone considered, although nowhere near as good as his brother. He was also given to strong drink.

Maxim had no interest in acting as a guide. *We don't want you to,* argued the salesman. *We just need you to come in with us.* Maxim had even less interest in that, although they began to hammer out a deal. Maxim's demands were new boots, two huge bottles of wine and twenty dollars. *All you have to do is come in with us,* the salesman persisted. *We don't want a guide. You'll just be a sport like us.*

They marched down to the air base, little Maxim held between them and snoring muzzily. *We have a guide,* they said, *and we want to go in.*

He's your guide?

They slapped Maxim's licence down onto the counter.

We want to go in.

And so they flew into the extreme.

They came out a few days later with four dressed fish that, together, weighed over thirty pounds.

The salesman from the Canada Needle and Fishing Tackle Company had landed an eleven-pound brookie on fly tackle.

ONE THING THIS STORY IS ABOUT IS MADNESS.

I don't mean to alarm anyone; I realize that you found this little volume in the section labelled "Fishing" in the bookstore. Or perhaps there wasn't a "Fishing" section at all, there was a "Sports" section, maybe even a "Leisure & Lifestyle." Whatever; I'm sure you didn't pull the book down from a cobwebbed shelf labelled "Lunacy," so it pains me to announce that one of its subjects is, um, madness. At the very least the appearance of madness, although when Gordon turned towards the north, a pasty-faced man made puffy by soiled, down-filled clothing, and bellowed, "Blow, you cocksucker, blow!", well, you needn't be much of a Shakespearean to be reminded of loony old Lear.

And I certainly appeared to be quite mad, one fine evening in early August of 1994. I was fishing in a Toronto city park. I do not mean that I was angling in, for example, High Park's Grenadier Pond, which some people do, people who are thought to be a little odd. No, there wasn't even any *water* where I was fishing. My older daughter was playing merrily on the nearby swing set, quite oblivious to the fact that the passersby thought her daddy was a madman, because there he stood, working a long fishing rod with, well, a certain level of dexterity. Which is to say, some of my casts were well executed. I would lay out a length of fly line behind me and then move my right arm forward, the wrist locked nicely. My left hand, holding line, would pull down suddenly and sharply. A tight little loop would curl out, slicing through the breeze, and land beautifully on the manicured lawn. Mind you, other casts were not so successful. Sometimes the tight little loop would be a huge-bellied billow, the fly line would be as much behind me as before, and this mess I would abort and crash-land, which usually had the effect of draping me indecorously with fly line and leader.

Meanwhile, strollers and air-takers would demand, "What are you fishing for?" and grin, each obviously claiming authorship of his or her cunning little jape.

I had devised a rueful rejoinder, to the effect that I didn't stand a significantly poorer chance here than I did on most of Ontario's lakes and streams. The rejoinder needed work and revision, of course, but was alarmingly close to the truth, given the sad shrivelling of our little blue world. If lakes are clean and crystal clear these days it means that acid rain has destroyed all the vegetation, it means that the fishes have nothing to eat, it means that you can flail a fly rod all day long and not elicit any piscine interest whatsoever. So any angling at all could, *should*, carry the stigma of madness. This gave me the little strength of character I needed to continue my casting in the city park.

What I was actually doing—and I would have happily told this to anybody who'd stopped to ask—was practising a technique called the Double Haul.

I'll tell you what that is—and in doing so introduce you more formally to Gordon—by recording the circumstances of my first seeing the cast demonstrated. It was in a public school gymnasium, ten summers before. A group of us, strangers to each other and variously aged, stood and watched a small man work a variety of fishing rods. He picked up a bait-casting rod, a plastic tear-shaped plug dangling from the end of the line, and fired it at a target at the other end of the room, perhaps eighty feet away. A red fire alarm dinged as the plug hit its geometric centre. Then he did the same thing with an open-faced casting reel. He next made the only woman present, his then-wife, stand in front of the target, her feet set wide apart. The plug hit the floor, skipped through the legs and made the fire alarm ding. I don't recall the little man saying much of anything as he demonstrated these things, although this seems unlikely in retrospect. He seemed to be going through the act in a hurry, as if anxious to move on to something else. He had his then-wife hold a half-peeled banana out to her side. The man picked up a fly rod and put the thick line into beautiful motion. Two or three slices of banana fell to the gymnasium floor. The little man hastily put the long pole aside and picked up a tiny one, a kind of dwarf fly rod.

The man, then entering his fifties, was short, slight in the limbs and a little potbellied. He owned wavy, greying hair that bobbed across his head in a spirited manner. With his silver hair and tanned face, he looked somehow Spanish. Not that I know many Spanish people, but I could imagine this man crouched on a beach somewhere on the Costa del Sol, mending a net with a needle fashioned from bone. (I was to find out he had a British—Cockney, to be exact—heritage. This made sense; it was even easier to imagine him in Dickens's filthy Londontown, hawking dace and bream in a thronged market.)

"The Double Haul," the man told us, "when well executed, can make any fly line go very far. I could make this fly line go a hundred feet." I did not understand much about casting in those days, but I understood that this was an extravagant boast, because he made the statement both extravagantly and boastfully. He took the tiny fly rod and worked it with great energy, first of all peeling bunches of line away and then casting with so much sudden force that he grunted like a weight lifter. The line flew away from the rod. It travelled easily ninety feet. "And it goes even farther," announced the little man, pointing at the floor beneath him, "when you're not standing on the running line."

The Double Haul was developed—a caster named Charles Ritz is credited with being the theoretician of the technique—so that a lot of line could be thrown, all at once, in order to cover a lot of water. I am not talking about the precise false-casting one associates with angling on a stream. I'm talking about a set of gross muscular actions, usually executed while a river tries to take your legs out from under you.

I can do it, that is, every now and again. Once I executed it flawlessly. This was at the North American Casting Championships, that year held in Cincinnatti. I was shooting a game called Angler's Fly, dependent on the technique. My timing was perfect, my balance and weight redistribution miraculous. (By which I mean that it's a miracle when I do something even vaguely graceful and athletic.) The line shot away towards heaven.

And then stopped abruptly, as I was standing on my running line.

One of the fine things about the Art of the Angle is that proselytes need initiation and guidance. I have a theory about the transitional nature of a human life, how one needs someone to facilitate passage, how this is often accomplished by an elder under the pretence of imparting the minutiae of some art or craft. When one decides upon fishing as a hobby, one has elected a lifetime of education. Some anglers, nearing the end of their days, have acquired vast knowledge, which they then share with the young ones. Fishing is an area that can, even in this decidedly unmagical day and age, still produce magi.

I call them "Old Guys."

The term is not intended to be disrespectful. I first heard it from the lips of Chris Korich, who at the time was competing in those same casting championships in Cincinnatti, finishing second that year to his archrival and long-time friend Steve Rajeff. I asked Chris how he learned his art. He described his first rod, which he found discarded on the bank of some stream. It had an old push-button closed-face spinning reel; the line trapped inside was densely knotted. Korich told me how he attached split-shot to the line in order to make a cast. This aberrant behaviour—the heavy shot would be uncontrollable and dangerously fast—was noticed by some old guys who took young Korich under their wings and showed him how to work the thing properly. These old guys were actually master casters at the Oakland Casting Club.

I have a vision of the young Korich standing by the casting pool, attended by the Old Guys. They are flaxen-haired, their faces weather-beaten and serene. They impart wisdom with forefingers aimed gently at heaven. "Oh no, Grasshopper," they speak gently. "Too much motion. The wrist must lock like a door against thieves."

That's the kind of Old Guy I wish I had.

I don't. I've got Gordon.

Immediately following his demonstration, the little man made his plans clear. He wanted to start a club. He already had a name devised; indeed, Gordon had cards and hats and designs for a nylon fishing jacket, all of which proclaimed the existence of the Scarborough Fly and Bait Casting Association. (I did not know at the time—and I did not find out without a certain amount of amateur sleuthing—that Gordon was in fact a dissenting renegade from the already established Toronto chapter of the American Casting Association.) Many of us, I think, were confused as to the proposed nature of this club. Clearly, fishing was involved, but it was not to be a fishing club per se. "We'll go on club trips," promised Gordon, "but this isn't about catching fish." That caused quite a few grumbles. "Basically," Gordon elucidated, "it's a tournament casting club."

I suspect many of you are unaware that the sport of tournament casting is alive and well both here and abroad. Its practitioners are few, but remarkably keen. They vie against each other on small ponds and manmade pools (these are the accuracy contests) and in huge flat fields (going for distance). That is what Gordon proposed to teach us, although he had other knowledge to share—how to tie flies, for example, and how to make bamboo fly rods.

Gordon's recruiting did not go especially well. One gentleman standing near me grumbled, "I just came to learn that Double Haul thing," and then walked away in some disgust when he learned that the knowledge of that one skill would cost him thirty bucks, the price of a year's membership in the club.

I eagerly ponied up the money. For one thing, I knew that the same knowledge was selling for thousands of dollars in upper state New York and Montana, in all the hallowed places of angling with a fly. For another, I was thirty years old, single, and felt I needed a new hobby, as my old one—drinking—was both expensive and a little hard on my health.

After the recruiting drive, Gordon showed some of his films. Gordon has a conception of himself as a filmmaker, working exclusively in the Super-8 format. He herded us—those of us who were interested in joining the club—into another room where a small projector was uncased and threaded up. Gordon went to the front of the room and pulled down the screen, and although this was presumably a chore often assigned to six- and seven-year-olds, Gordon had some trouble executing it. The screen refused to stay down, refurling and flapping whenever he released the silver ring. Gordon often has problems like this, where he is baffled and undone by simple examples of humankind's invention. He solved this problem in typical fashion, fetching the butt end of a casting rod, then fixing one end through the ring, the other through a chair. Someone suggested to him that there was a trick to the thing, that an emphatic jerk when the screen was extended triggered a locking mechanism. Gordon shrugged, appraised his jerry-rigging and found it to be good.

He switched off the lights and started the projector.

The colour was washed out, because the film was many years old. The hand that held the camera was steady enough, but the operator seemed overly excited, and there was plenty of sick-making motion as he tried to record the whole glorious world.

Most of that world was river. It was unlike any I'd ever seen, because I'd only seen sedate rivers in southern Ontario, most of which were reliable employees of the government, working for the canal systems. Some of them might actually have been wider than the river in the film; many carried more water. But none seemed to be coming from the top of the globe. None had this river's rambunctiousness, the water white and foamy as it galloped over and between boulders. The explosion of current and rock resulted in the rest of the world being mist and rainbow.

"That's the Broadback River," said Gordon, supplying the commentary for the silent film.

There was a cut and we saw a youngish man holding a rod bent hard towards the tumult. "That's Jurgen," said Gordon. "He's fighting a world-record fish there." Jurgen's rod, in the film, went suddenly limp, that is, it popped up horizontal. "Jurgen just lost a world-record fish," noted Gordon.

The film then cut to the image of a campsite. Men sat about in long underwear. One of them, his face lathered copiously, stood in front of a tree where a small hand mirror was fixed with a nail. He scraped away whiskers and seemed to be whistling. Another man worked at an improvised fly-tying table, his little vise screwed onto the side of a packing crate. The sunlight threatened to wash away all of these images.

Another quick cut and we were in the bow of a canoe, which was headed upriver in a steady way. There was another cut and we saw that it was a long canoe, that it easily carried three people, that it sported an old white Johnson motor on the back end. (It is this sort of thing that reinforced Gordon's notion of himself as a filmmaker. When you think about it, he'd obviously stopped the trek and demanded to be put out on the side of the river so that he could film this intercut. His mates likely obeyed glumly, anxious to arrive at the fishing grounds.)

Then we saw a man catch a fish. It took some minutes, the man waving his rod as though it were a baton and he was conducting a marching band very far away. He ultimately fought the fish to submission, the creature finning in a small pool, exhausted and whipped. Another man stepped into the river and raised the fish into the air. Even given the agedness of the film, the fish was brilliantly and beautifully coloured.

I will return abruptly to the city park, and hope that you accept this temporal to-ing and fro-ing. The motion of the fly line acts as a metaphor, for as any caster can tell you, what happens behind you is just as important as what happens in front. That's why the evening in early August is such a wonderful place to begin, coming after my education with Gordon but before the trip.

I was practising the Double Haul because my command of the technique was imperfect to begin with, and rusty from years of discontinuance. And I was soon leaving to fish a big river that was said to be full of big fish. "For when sleeping I dream of big fish and strong fights," wrote Theocritus in *The Fisherman's Dream*, "just as a dog dreams of chasing bears." Even this was not sufficient for my Old Guy, who dreamt of taking the *biggest* fish out of the river, thereby earning himself a nickel's worth of immortality.

It was Gordon's stated aim to catch a world-record speckled trout.

The current world record, as was noted by our salesman from the prologue, is fourteen and a half pounds. That fish was taken from Ontario's Nipigon River, in the year 1916. The angler, a Dr. Cook, had been using live bait.

The fish's skin was removed from its body and shellacked. This shiny husk was then placed over a log to suggest girth, and that curious display was toured across Canada for many years. It often showed up at train stations, and it was at the depot in Port Arthur that the young Gordon first set eyes upon it. His father had to physically haul him away lest they miss their train. His father was a famous radio personality, and toured his show across Canada during the summer. He was always in a hurry to catch the next train, so Gordon had only a few moments to gawk at Dr. Cook's fish.

Somewhere in those moments Gordon determined that he would one day catch a bigger speckled trout.

If you read Ernest Schwiebert's magnum opus *Trout*—which is housed in two volumes and over a thousand pages long—you will learn that the next world-record speckled trout will come from one of two places. One is Argentina, where the fish was transplanted some years ago. The other is northern Quebec, where mighty rivers like the Broadback pound into James Bay. Part of the Broadback watershed is made up of the huge Lac Assinica.

You might wonder what there is about northern Quebec that makes it a likely breeding ground for an enormous speckled—also called a brook—trout. Again I refer to the pages of *Trout*. (Schwiebert not only wrote the thing, he illustrated it, and very well, too. The two volumes contain everything that you ever wanted to know about the fish, and much that you didn't; it is an awe-inspiring piece of work, and very humbling to me and my little volume. I am, perhaps, going to draw a picture later on, so as not to feel too shamefaced.) Schwiebert points out that "good brookie water has narrowly defined limits of chemistry and physical character." The brook trout demands icy cold rivers and lakes. Well, we got that, by god. Not just in Quebec, either; Canada possesses some of the largest *archaeocene* outcroppings in the world, which means that our land was made six hundred million years ago, and has just been sitting there ever since, so our water's plenty cold enough for speckled trout.

But there is another force at work, a peculiar moulding, a mutation, of the Assinica strain of fish. For one thing, they seem to be longer-lived, extending the fish's normal four-year life span by perhaps six additional years. They are also temperamentally different. Well, I should respeak myself. It is not necessary for you to believe, as I do, that fish have temperaments. There are *behavioural* differences. Schwiebert describes an experiment in trout-rearing, domestic fishes and the Assinica strain reared side by side. *Les truites* were generally smaller, but more active. Significantly—in light of the story I'm about to tell—the American trouts, spotting a lab worker nearing the tanks, would rush over expecting food. *Les truites* hid.

When the fish were transplanted into a test stream, the mortality rate was much lower for the Assinica fish.

Mortality is an important factor here.

One day, in the cold, cold winter of 'ninety-four, Gordon sent me a letter. He holds the medium of the letter in somewhat antiquated esteem. Important thoughts, adventures and ideas are always set down on paper and disseminated, to friends and club members, through the mail. This particular letter had a tone of giddy enthusiasm. Gordon wanted to go to northern Quebec. He'd been there before—eleven times over thirty years—but the world-record brook trout had ever eluded him. Twice, Gordon pointed out in his letter, though it was information I knew well, he'd had the fish on his line, but ill luck and frayed leaders had deprived him of his place in the annals. *One more time,* Gordon wrote. He wanted to go back one more time, and he was therefore mounting an expedition.

Can I count on you, Paul?

I folded up the page very neatly, replaced it in the envelope and put the letter somewhere my wife was not likely to find it.

The simple answer was no. I was no longer thirty years old and single, I was forty years old and familied. I had managed to cobble together an unlikely career, selling lies and fancy to publishers and movie producers. When your stock in trade is lies and fancy, there is always a real possibility of the market disappearing. This is what I felt, at any rate, so I would take all the work that was offered. This rendered me distracted and distant and often had me banging on the computer in the middle of the night. Still, I needed the career because I had a family, which included, at the time, a little female child and a brand-new baby one. So I was too damn busy to go traipsing off to northern Quebec with Gordon.

The telephone rang. This was seven, eight minutes after I'd put down the letter.

"Hello?"

"What do you say, Kew?" (I'll render it that way—Gordon actually calls me "Q", originally to avoid confusion with another club member also named Paul.)

"Well, I don't know."

"Awww, you gotta come, man!"

Gnawing at me, if we can call a slight gall a gnaw, was the knowledge that Gordon didn't just want me to come, he *needed* me. I had a sideline to my lies and fancy business, journalism. (Not the likeliest extension, I know, but one does what one can.) The expedition required money—actually quite a bit of money—and Gordon thought that I might be able to raise the funds by securing a contract with a magazine to publish our adventures.

There is a great tradition of this, of course. An example that springs to mind comes from a wonderful book entitled *Great Heart: The History of a Labrador Adventure*. (It was written by James West Davidson and John Rugge, by the way, published in 1988 by Viking.)* The book was recommended to me by Gordon, who reported that, having started to read, he eschewed all normal activity—eating, sleeping, etc.—until he finished the book.

Great Heart tells the true story of a man named Leonidas Hubbard, a junior editor at something called *Outing* magazine at the turn of the century. Hubbard, hoping to "make his reputation," proposed to his senior that he make a trek across Labrador. He said that he would keep a journal and, upon his safe return, compose a detailed account of the days spent in the wilderness. His editor at *Outing*, a man named Caspar Whitney, said okay, but only grudgingly. He lacked the word in his vocabulary back then, but he thought Hubbard's idea was pretty *whuss*. Canoeing across Labrador in the middle of summer was nothing—Whitney had made his reputation by snowshoeing two thousand miles across the Northwest Territories.

*Reissued in paperback in 1996 by Kodansha America.

What happens to Hubbard I'll tell in time. For now I will only use him as an exemplar of this thought, that to make one's reputation is a very seductive notion. I had a reputation, I suppose, but not as a fishing writer. With a reputation as a fishing writer, I could, I don't know, attend literary conferences on "Deconstructionism and the Carp." Magazines like *Outing* would pay me to go to far-flung places and test the waters. I would have the opportunity to fish more, and I love to fish.

That simple fact also factored into my thinking. I love to fish, though there never seemed to be enough time, and what time there was was spent upon rivers and lakes where there were too many anglers and not enough fish. We seem to be ruining the world—I am not learned enough to say exactly how, I only have my observational evidence, i.e., the fish are no longer there. I am also not going to point my finger at fat-butted industrialists and accuse them of poisoning the water. I won't let them off the hook, but I've seen pictures, we've all seen pictures, of our young gap-toothed grandfathers posing beside crude wooden structures decorated with the corpses of two hundred fish.

And I'll tell you something else, something that I didn't tell my wife even as I described the potential professional rewards to be had by my abandoning her and the children for a couple of weeks in August. I didn't tell her that I'd wanted to go ever since I saw those little Super-8 movies, that first night I'd met my Old Guy.

Gordon began a campaign of letter writing. The correspondence that ensued between him and the Quebec government is now contained in a folder about two inches thick. I have been through it many times, but it's mind-boggling bureaucratic stuff, made all the more deadly by suspect translation on both sides. Gordon relished the paper battle, calling me often during its raging and exclaiming, "By god, Kew, there's a whole chapter's worth right here!"

Don't worry, I wouldn't do that to you. I can reduce it to the essence, but before I do, I must tell you about the Old Place.

The Old Place is a small island in the Broadback River. It is only technically an island; it sits hard by the shore and rocks pepper the water, silently beckoning one across. The island plugs the river, divides the water, so on either side there are rapids. Not so big as to be dangerous, just big enough to be full of fish. One can walk to other fishing grounds, including a magical little waterfall where great big squaretails go to shower. And, should one tire of the wonderful angling, the Old Place affords an ideal launching pad for a motorized canoe, upstream or downstream to new adventure.

Gordon found the Old Place thirty years ago. This is where he's returned again and again, bringing various friends with him. Gordon can't distinguish trips by year; he can only try to recall who was there with him: *Was it Don and Pete? Or was it Jack and Gary and Carl?*

One thing is clear and certain—Gordon loves the Old Place more than any other real estate God has ever come up with. And the first thing the Quebec government told him was that he couldn't go back there.

It seems that Hydro-Québec had driven into the north of the land, there to lash and tether the mighty rivers, to put them to the slavish work of producing energy.

Even before it became clear that we were going to go, even during that period when we felt mummified by red tape, I began to make preparations.

There is a store in Toronto called Skinner Sports that services the fly fisher's every need. One day, I took myself down there to buy some Despairs. These are Gordon's favourite flies, and he has taught me how to make them, but my efforts always seemed tawdry and askew. I could have put up with this—all of my hand-tied flies are tawdry and askew—but to make a Despair it is necessary to take two conjoined filaments of peacock herl and put a half hitch in the middle. Fat fingers and middle-aged eyes aren't the best tools for this operation. So although Gordon viewed the practice with massive disdain, whenever I wanted Despairs I just went and bought a bunch.

The young man behind the counter asked me where I was going fishing. When I told him, he asked with whom. When I answered that, he asked "Why?"

Apparently the young man knew my Old Guy.

The young man pointed towards a colleague. "He's just been up fishing on the Broadback."

"Oh, yeah?" Common practice and courtesy demanded that I turn towards the colleague and ask, "How did you do?"

"Terrible."

"Ah!"

"You know what? You know what?" the colleague demanded, with terrible urgency informing his voice. "The Quebec government has totally destroyed the land up there. They're doing stuff, man, it's science fiction stuff. They have *turned rivers around.*"

"What do you mean?"

"Turned 'em around. Reversed them. Made them flow the other way."

This may or may not be true—a documentarian working on a film about the Great Whale project assured me that it was so—but Hydro-Québec was undeniably up there. That was the explanation behind the government's first refusal to let us go in.

Because of Hydro's presence, and the hundreds of workers that entailed, the province had called a moratorium on fishing for one year. They didn't want the workers depleting the stock of pickerel, so they simply called a halt to the whole activity. Except if you were *un sport*, and wanted to go to one of the two camps that were in the area.

Gordon had absolutely no desire to go to one of the two camps. In trying to explain himself, he used an expression I hadn't heard since the sixties, that he wanted to "do his own thing." He fired back a series of letters: *Think of the publicity that will accrue to the province,* he argued, *when we catch the world's largest speckled trout. Think of the tourism that's going to bring in. It's not like we're going to hurt anything,* he pleaded. *We'll just go to the Old Place and fish happily and no one will ever see us.*

Confusing the issue was the fact that the PQ bureaucrats kept passing the buck and the ball, and Gordon was never quite sure with whom he was dealing. Eventually they agreed to let us go fishing, but we had to get the permission of one of the two guys who ran camps. Gordon knew both men, a White, a Demers. White he didn't think would help, which I took to mean that Gordon and White had history. Gordon now abandoned his little typewriter and took up his other instrument of communication, the telephone. Demers, he discovered, came out of the bush once a week to attend to chores in Chibougamau. *Have him call me,* Gordon told Demers's sister, and then there were days of waiting. When Demers called, he was suspicious. He accused Gordon of being in league with the Quebec government: this was all some trick; if Demers authorized fishing where no fishing should be done, the province would come and shut him down. Gordon began talking, and when he was done, he had Demers's permission.

He told the government. They said *Bien. You have permission to fish anywhere within Demers's territory.* They sent a map, a perfect circle imposed on the geography. It came achingly close to, but did not include, the Old Place.

We held a planning session, the four of us.

Gordon felt it necessary to have four men on the journey, both to lighten various workloads and to make a more balanced, equitable little society. He assembled the expedition with all the forethought of an assault on Everest, choosing men because of their singular expertise and talents.

I was the scribe, of course. Or at least I thought I was. After all, I packed three spanking new notebooks and a quiver of felt-tipped pens into my knapsack. My intention was to record every happenstance and detail, making my notebooks dense with poetry. I'd signed a contract with a fine house to publish the account, and had hopes of producing a volume of such substance that even Ernie Schwiebert would be impressed.

Gordon was the cook and guide, despite the fact that he didn't possess any sense of direction. Gordon's lack of a sense of direction was rather extraordinary given the outdoorsy nature of his life. Once, driving through a town in a westerly direction, he was forced to take a short detour, a block up a street running north. Gordon sat at the stop sign and deliberated for a couple of minutes, looking first right, then left, back again, etc., until I screamed (this was an early-morning fishing trip; I can tell because I seem so damn cranky), "Left! Left!"

Gordon shrugged, as though he couldn't understand why I was making such a big deal out of this. He threw on his signal indicator, even though the world was deserted, and very carefully executed the turn.

Paulo was a young Portuguese man, six-foot-two and beefy. He had thick black hair and an even thicker black moustache. He had served in the Portuguese Air Force, working as a mechanic on airplanes and helicopters, so his official area of expertise was the repair and maintenance of machinery. Paulo was also there because of his unrestrained delight in all things piscatorial. When he caught a fish he would bellow "Yahooo!" with ear-splitting intensity. This excitement possessed an afterlife of several hours, during which he'd recount the taking of the beast many times. Gordon allowed as how Paulo would be invaluable if spirits needed raising. Gordon hadn't considered, I don't think, that with Paulo's boyish enthusiasm came a corresponding despair, a hopelessness, when things didn't go well—but I'm getting ahead of myself in the story here.

Gary was as sobersided as Paulo was manic-depressive. He was a professional guitarist and as such possessed an excellent sense of humour and a vast repertoire of jokes (orchestra pits are where jokes go to get born), but his demeanour was very possessed and sensible. Gary was the most experienced camper, having made numerous canoe trips through the brush, but he had only one official function: dishwashing. "It's a chance for me to get my hands warm," he'd told us, when asking, politely, if anyone had any objections to his doing all the dishes. Gary was a veteran of these trips and seemed to have some idea that it might get a bit chilly up there.

We spread a map of the area over Gary's coffee table and examined it. It showed an intricate assemblage of waterways, some connecting, some dead ends, a huge maze designed by psychologists to madden laboratory rats. There were elevation lines everywhere, short and sloppily angled, so that this world appeared to have been stitched together by Dr. Frankenstein.

It looked quite easy to get lost up there. That fellow from the book *Great Heart* did, by the way, Leonidas Hubbard and his mate, Wallace, and their Indian guide, George. When the rivers and lakes of the extreme north proved too confusing, they abandoned their canoes and went overland, hoping to reconnect up with the main waterway. They missed spotting it by a couple of hundred yards. They ran out of food.

"We're not going to run out of food, are we?" I demanded suddenly.

Gary and Gordon gave me strange looks, because our immediate aim was to find a suitable spot to camp and fish. I managed to alarm Paulo with this thought, though, and as the two of us fretted, Gary and Gordon, spectacles balanced on the ends of noses, pored over the map.

The Old Place lay a quarter of an inch beyond the circle marking Demers's territory. Every time Gary or Gordon glanced at that section of the map they'd shake their heads mournfully.

"Here." Gary placed a finger on the map. "There's a small lake here," by which he referred to a widening of the river that connected Lac Assinica to the Broadback. "And then an island here, dividing the water. There'd be rapids on either side. And if need be, we could either go south to these rapids here—" He moved his finger until it was pointed at some slash marks. "Or these up here."

Gordon stared at the map intently. "It looks good," he said uncertainly.

"Why don't we just go to the place where you have fished so many times before?" demanded Paulo. Gordon, I saw, was his Old Guy as well, and the young man had heard the stories many, many times.

"They won't fly us there," said Gordon. "They know we're not allowed to go there."

"Because," persisted Paulo, "it's not really very good, to go to a place that no one knows. Suppose there's nothing there to catch but pike?"

Paulo held that species in massive disdain, a stance adopted from Gordon. I myself am rather fond of angling for pike, a bone of contention between Gordon and myself. But we've learned to live with such bones. "They'd be huge pike," I pointed out.

"Gordon," said Paulo urgently, "tell me this. Would you eat a pike?"

Gordon wrinkled his nose and obligingly made a sour face.

"No, but seriously, tell me," persisted Paulo. "Would you eat a pike?" It seemed to be a matter of some import to Paulo.

"No," allowed Gordon. Paulo exhaled with deep satisfaction. "But don't worry about that," said the Old Guy. "There's going to be plenty of speckled trout. You want to come home with a mountie, Paulo?"

"Yes, that is what I want. Not too big a fish, just a nice one to hang on my wall."

"You're going to catch one."

"Ah!"

"And if I don't catch the world record, I hope one of you does."

"Ah!" Only Paulo responded. Gary was cleaning his rec room, gathering up pop bottles and chip debris. I stared at the map, hoping to make sense out of the cartographical confusion.

Gordon pointed a trembling finger—his fingers always trembled slightly—at the small widening of water. "We're calling this," he announced grandly, "Q Lake."

The trip began late on a summer's eve, it being our plan to avoid both heat and other motorists by cruising through the long night.

I will do away with the hours spent in Gordon's car, hours spent hunched and twisted, four of us and several wooden packing crates sharing ten linear feet of velour-covered foam rubber. I will open this scene in the middle of the action, although there is not that much action to speak of.

We were hanging around Propair on a spectacular day in late August. The little airport lay just to the south of Chibougamau, situated on the side of Lac Cache. I was amusing myself with, alternately, doing the *New York Times* crossword puzzle and throwing a stick for an addled-looking dog. It might be seen as some sort of omen that the dog, upon first setting its teeth in retrieval, would beat the shit out of the stick, banging it on the ground in a frantic attempt to render it more senseless than it already was.

Gordon and Paulo were in town fetching the rented canoe. Gary was sitting on one of the plane's jump seats with a small journal opened on his lap. He was working at it with great concentration and industry. Occasionally he would glance up, chew at his pen with poetic pensiveness and then set upon his paper once again. *What the hell could he be writing,* I wondered, *detailed descriptions of the individual trees?*

I felt vaguely guilty. A more responsible journalist would have scribbled something down, but my notebooks were all stowed away, which means that to write anything down I would have had to tunnel through a mountain of luggage.

Speaking of this luggage (though part of me is tempted to not get started on this subject), Gordon had long ago told us that there would be a weight restriction on the airplane. Given the projected tonnage of the fishing and camping equipment, the food, etc., Gordon told us that we each had a personal restriction of twenty-five pounds. He then handed me a list of everything I needed to bring. It was easily a hundred pounds' worth. Take a look:

4 shirts	3 pair heavy-weight socks
1 jack shirt	2 pair suspenders
2 T-shirts	1 belt
2 pair pants	1 lightweight jacket
2 sets long johns	(or windbreaker)
4 Jockey shorts	1 down vest
3 pair medium-weight socks	1 down parka

1 fishin' hat
1 rain suit
1 head net
1 set waders (preferably
   felt-soled)
1 set leather boots
1 set lightweight lined boots
1 pair mukluks or moccasins
1 set hip boots or
   rubber boots
2 sets work gloves
1 wool toque
towel and facecloth

toothbrush
face soap
1 fly rod
1 fly reel
1 spare spool
1 spinning rod
1 spinning reel
1 spare spool
3 dozen assorted Mepps
   or Vibrax
assorted flies
1 w.f.s. fly line
1 w.f.f. fly line

(The w.f.s. and w.f.f. distinction above is between lines that sink and lines that float. Both lines are weight-forward, tapered so as to be more substantial near the head. I might have indicated this simply enough by expanding the initials, but I'm sure we all felt the need for a little break. Break's over.)

spare fly-line leaders
fly-tying vice
nylon-covered fish stringer
landing net
camera and film
fishermen's pliers
hook hone
fishing vest
life jacket
pocketknife

small flashlight
waterproof matches
pocket compass
Band-Aids
boot hanger
Kleenex pack
razor and shaving cream
small mirror
personal medicines
comb and brush

Muskol
sleeping bag (in high-
density garbage bag)
pillow
cot and mattress
Polaroid glasses
reading glasses
(if necessary)

wading staff
50 feet strong nylon cord
Bic lighter
pocket scale and rule
book or magazine
handkerchiefs
travel alarm and watch

I had done my best to scavenge all the necessary gear, but not without some radical rethinking. It occurred to me that I only had the two feet, for example, and could not understand why I had to bring so much damn footwear. Lugging along both hip waders and chest waders seemed excessive—you understand that the chest waders perforce went up over my hips—so I was able to lose a few pounds there.

Gordon called one day. "You don't have to bring everything on the list," he told me.

"Okay, good."

"Paulo's got work gloves for all of us."

"Oh?"

"Yeah. And I got a bag of Bic lighters."

"Excellent. There's a few ounces of overage I don't have to worry about. The sixty-seven pounds is still a bit of a headache."

"Oh!" he said as his memory kicked in. "I forgot something on that list."

"You *did*?"

"A whistle."

"Whistle?"

"For communication over great distances."

I was able to condense my personal belongings, rolling them, bundling them, until they fit into a backpack that I'd borrowed from Janet across the road. This backpack, a well-made and cleverly designed thing, had been to Nepal. I had a waterproof gym bag in which I placed the rest of my stuff. That, plus a sleeping bag and a sack that held pens, note-books, tape recorder, Walkman, etc., etc., was all I had. It may sound like a lot. It did weigh in excess of twenty-five pounds, I'll admit that.

Paulo's socks alone weighed in excess of twenty-five pounds.

He had two huge duffle bags that I think might explain how the ancient Egyptians carried rock to the site of the Great Pyramids. This is not counting his sleeping roll, sim-ilarly oversized. Gary was not quite so bad, and at least had the good grace to feel guilty, staring at his mound of luggage and tsking his tongue in a doleful manner. Gordon you couldn't fault, because he carried much that was to the general good, and he tried to be as compact as possible, largely through an intricate system of lashing and folding that involved pieces of exploded inner tube.

There was also the collapsible boat, a strange piece of equipment that Gordon held an unwarranted affection for. "I can have it ready to go in less than forty seconds. Time me." He could never really accomplish the task in anything under about five minutes, pulling apart the long metallic lips, leaping inside and grappling with various stays and sheaths. The point being, the thing weighed quite a bit. We were clearly overweight, which I wouldn't have seen as that big a problem were it not for a picture, snipped out of a magazine, Scotch-taped to the wall of the little airport. "This airplane," read the caption, "was two hundred pounds overweight before it took off." Of course, there was no airplane in the picture, only a tiny pile of smoking crumple.

Gordon assumed that, as in previous trips, the pilot would put everything on a scale before filling up the airplane's belly. We had all been advised to mentally preselect items for exclusion. I hadn't done that: first, because I was the closest to twenty-five pounds to begin with; second, because I had already made the supreme sacrifice—I was bringing no beer.

A car screamed into the parking lot, from which leapt Richard Demers, a man in unlikely dress—leather pants and vest, snakeskin boots—with a complexion like a bowling alley wipe-rag and a voice so gravelly that he seemed demonically possessed. "*Il a,*" he bellowed, "*la permission spéciale!!*" This was addressed mostly to the woman who hurried along behind him, red-faced with the exertion required to trail her husband, but it was also a loud, sneering complaint to the gods. They disappeared into the airport, or whatever you choose to call the small building with the large map of the northern extreme pinned to the wall. I continued my crossword puzzle. Gary continued making notes. From inside the airport came short bursts of derisive laughter. Demers's bray was the loudest, and, judging from the harsh rumbling that preceded each round, he was also precipitating most of it. I hoped he was telling jokes that he'd heard in the bar—it was more than obvious that the bar was where he'd just been— but I knew he was laughing at us.

Gordon and Paulo returned with the War Canoe. It was a huge Larivée, the stern blunted so that one could mount an outboard motor. Oh, yeah, I forgot to mention that we had an outboard motor. This is what the entire packing procedure was like, by the way. *Oh, yeah, I forget to mention that we have an outboard motor, let me just throw it in the backseat here between you and Paulo.* This was a very interesting outboard motor, especially from the historical point of view. It bore the brand name Johnson, but I suspected this referred to, say, Ebediah Johnson, or whichever patriach first conceived of the steam-driven propeller. Actually the machine was only forty years old, younger than me, and like all of Gordon's contraptions, it had been kept in working fettle. More to the point, Gordon had refused to let it die, keeping it in the vale with elastic bands and bobby pins.

So Paulo and Gordon arrived with the War Canoe, which they added to the luggage we had piled on the deck beside the Otter. It didn't contribute significantly.

Richard Demers swaggered out onto the airport porch (now *there* are two words I never thought I'd put together) and hollered, "Come here and talk to me."

Gordon hurried along, Paulo hard on his heels. Gary and I followed somewhat reluctantly—Gary because he was loath to abandon his work, I because, well, I just had a bad feeling about the whole enterprise.

There was a map of the territory spread out over the counter. Demers had his elbows pinning the corners, as if holding it down against a raging wind. His eyes ravaged the thing. Gordon held a finger down upon it, obscuring the tiny island in the river system that he wanted Demers to see. "I think the plane can land here," Gordon said, showing where the water of Q Lake ballooned out before the isle.

"No," said Demers. "Dat's full of rocks."

Noticing the three of us standing behind our Old Guy, Demers pushed himself up to his full standing height and announced, "I smoke, I drink and I fuck."

"Oh yes, nice to meet you, too."

Demers recollapsed upon the map. "Dis island," he told Gordon, "is *wild*."

Gordon's eyes narrowed.

Demers, hunched and now permanently cross-eyed from staring at the map, moved his finger about an inch to the east, a distance of perhaps seven miles upriver. "Here is where I used to have a camp," he told us. "This was eight year ago, so dere's nothing dere now. But it's second-growth. Dis island you want," he repeated, "is *wild*. And look, dere's a nice creek flow out right here. It's got some nice trout. Eight, maybe nine pound." He turned towards me suddenly and winked, at any rate performed some stunt with his bleary eyes that demonstrated autonomy, and announced, "We don't count all de two-, tree-pounders."

"Richard," said a very sombre Gordon.

"Gordon?"

"As you know, we have a specific purpose here."

"I know dat, yes."

"Now, look at the way this island—"

"Dat island is *wild*. And dat water is full of rocks."

Gordon became suddenly nostalgic, for no reason that I could fathom. "I came here when your father ran the camp," he said.

Demers nodded, as if willing to grant a philosophic point.

"He was a character," said Gordon.

Richard Demers seemed to take this as a challenge. "I smoke, I drink and I fuck," he announced once more. "Not like you," he sneered towards Gordon. "You're too *old* to fuck."

Gordon laughed. Demers laughed and deposited something unseemly on the ground, then reached into his back pocket and pulled out various forms, and the conversation involving our destination seemed to be forgotten. "I can give you da camping permit," he said, "but you'll have to get your licences in town."

"But you said you'd have the licences."

"You have to get them in town," he repeated, so off we went, which meant that by the time we returned it had just gone four o'clock. That very long day was marching towards its end.

We helped the pilot load the Otter. He did this without comment or complaint, merely accepted everything we handed him and threw it into the cargo area. He registered nothing as we handed him canoes, engines and collapsible boats. When everything was packed and stowed, the pilot appraised the load. I was kind of hoping that he'd abort the mission. Hadn't he seen that photograph taped to the airport wall, the one of the plane that had been a mere two hundred pounds overweight? Either of Paulo's duffle bags was two hundred pounds overweight. "I'll be right back," said the pilot, and he jumped from the plane, leapt into a nearby truck and roared off towards Chibougamau.

Ten minutes later he returned and gently added a case of beer to the top of the pile. "That's mine for later," he said, smiling.

Then we lit out for the territories.

Paulo asked to sit up front with the pilot. The pilot agreed, probably responding to something endearingly childlike in Paulo, or perhaps simply to the way the man was dressed, in shorts and a T-shirt featuring Disney characters.

I sat in one of the little jump seats. I did not feel well. I think in retrospect that I hadn't been feeling well for months, but only in those moments preceding takeoff was I willing to admit this to myself. I was filled with a clammy dread, which I put down to the fact that I was sitting on a small aircraft that was two tons overweight (two tons and a case of fucking beer) and about to perish.

Gordon turned around and handed me two plugs of yellow foam rubber. The plane was taxiing out to the middle of the lake, and the noise it produced was too loud to speak over. Gordon therefore gesticulated, showing how I should knead and mould the foam rubber until it was of a size and shape to plug my ears. I shook my head. I wasn't about to be found under a pile of steaming crumple with two bolts of foam rubber sticking out of my ears. Gordon shrugged and turned around in his seat. He put his hands on his knees and giggled; his entire body shook with barely contained excitement.

Suddenly the plane was racing across the lake. The noise was deafening. I frantically crammed foam rubber into my ears. The tree line on the shore opposite approached with alarming speed. Then we lifted off, although the sensation was that of the earth dropping away, being sucked out from underneath. The aircraft ascended slowly, the wings teetering like a wirewalker's balancing pole. I was smiling, but truly I was just trying to save the undertaker some work, setting my own features in a bland and artificially pleasant way.

The scenery below was glorious, or so I determined once I managed to open my eyes, which was perhaps ten minutes into the flight. Below me spread a blanket of water and land. The flatness was interrupted here and there by the occasional swollen belly of earth, perhaps with a manmade structure clinging desperately to its side; otherwise the expanse was perfect and endless. Except that it was lacerated twice by dirt roads and hydro towers, tearing through the land with mathematical precision.

How we'd arranged it was thus: the pilot had agreed to take us to our spot. He was going to circle the little island. This would give the pilot an opportunity to judge just how rock-filled Q Lake was. Meanwhile, Gordon would be looking at the island, seeking suitable camping spots. He would judge the rapids that framed it for fishability. We still had the opportunity to abort this first place, to redirect the pilot upstream and land near Richard Demers's abandoned outpost.

As the pilot began to circle the island, I saw right away there was a flaw in this plan: there would be no discussion about where to land, not unless we became very accomplished mimes very quickly. The sound inside the plane was deafening, besides which, the pilot wore padded ear mufflers, besides which, Gordon was paying no attention to him. Gordon was standing up, his face pressed against the oval of thick plastic on the side of the plane, staring down at the island. Gary remained sitting but looked out his own porthole, and quite visibly dismissed what he saw. He later told me he was sure that Gordon would at any time tap the pilot on the shoulder and waggle a finger towards the west. But the pilot continued drawing the circle tighter, lowering towards the earth, and Gordon continued staring through the window.

And then the pilot was making his final approach, finding a safe course through what was indeed rock-studded, fairly shallow water. He turned the plane around and backed up, bumping the rear of the floats against brown brush and tangle.

Soon we found ourselves upon what we came to know as Murphy's Island.

This was a wonderful feeling. Those of you who don't fish will not understand. Those of you who do will remember staring at the pages of *Field & Stream* in the bleak midwinter, your heart filled with exquisite yearning. You stare at a photograph of an angler out in the remote, out in the extreme, and you would for a moment give anything to be there with him.

I was finally in a photograph from *Field & Stream*.

I hadn't been all that keen on fishing when I was a youngster. Our family would rent cottages on various lakes, and I can recall angling with my father and brothers. I suppose I evidenced a certain enthusiasm, getting agitated and giddy whenever I caught a small sunfish, urging my boatmates to keep any and all sunfish hooked, the reason being that I liked to eat them. I understand now my father's looks of weariness as the bottom of the boat filled with flipping bluegills, because he would have to clean them all, fry them up and feed them to his chubby little son.

I can't remember fishing at all as a teen-ager. There were many times when I was in the North, close to water, close to fish, but I had other things on my mind, chiefly pharmaceuticals. In my twenties I was a rock-and-roll musician, and even though that job took me across some of the finest angling water on the continent, I only fished once. Four of us rented a little boat on Vancouver Island and went off in search of salmon. We found none; we found something called a dogfish, a skanky little shark. I found that experience vaguely off-putting, so I thought no more about fishing until some friends of mine purchased Wolverine Lodge.

Wolverine Lodge is a semidilapidated hulk of a hotel that sits on the lower branch of the Magnetawan River, just to the north of Parry Sound (the home of Bobby Orr), Ontario. The passenger train once came within a mile of the lodge's doors, and during the 1920s it was a fashionable getaway for railway magnates, honeymooners and nimrods. When the passenger lines were done away with, Wolverine Lodge ceased to be a profitable business, so it was purchased by a consortium, like-minded sorts with enough fond memories of the sixties to believe that people can get along with each other if given half a chance.

The Magnetawan River has some decent fishing. In one of the drawers behind the check-in desk, we found some yellowed pamphlets advertising the lodge. There were various pictures of the nimrods. They hunkered on rocks—the dead bodies of pickerel and bass arranged artfully all about them—and grinned like idiots. We went out onto the river in boats. We figured out how to angle for pickerel. I learned something resembling conservation; I couldn't eat all the pickerel I caught, the way I could sunfish, so many were slipped gently back into their home.

Big bullying bass made themselves known to me, piggy brutes that danced on top of the water and screamed a silent "Fuck you!" These were fun to catch, though not to eat particularly, so I became a catch-and-release fisherman.

Some of my friends, perhaps gentler souls than I, have ethical problems with this. I truly believe that fish don't experience pain in the same way humans do, that while a hooked upper lip may cause them alarm and distress, it is not, well, painful. If I truly thought the fish was experiencing pain, if it convulsed and let loose awful ululations across the water, I wouldn't be able to angle. Neither would a great many people, is my belief. "Look," I once suggested to my friend the Professor, "you could do the same thing with birds, correct? You could thread a worm on a hook, toss it on the lawn and wait for some little robin or blue jay to pop it down its throat. Now, why do you think people don't do that?"

"Because," answered the Professor, "it hasn't occurred to them yet."

My parents have a house in the country, in the gentle rolling land around Port Hope. There is a large pond on the property, the size of two football fields placed end to end. At one end is a dam; below the dam is a small creek that makes its way out to Lake Ontario.

I spent some of my thirtieth year there, mostly due to severe poverty. I was also being pretty severe as regards my personal life and habits, and I found the Pond a verdant asylum.

One morning I arose around five-thirty, slipped long-johned legs into chilly hip waders and went out into the world.

The Pond was contained in a large earth-bowl. I could see nothing but an oval of light-pocked sky, the stars being shooed away by a flickering wash of sun from the east. My little spinning rod was hoist across my shoulder, my hip waders whistled musically in the dew. I felt very virtuous, as I usually do when I'm up at five-thirty in the morning, except of course if I've sneaked up on it and am hailing the dawn with a large porcelain loudspeaker.

I heard a small noise, a distant barking. I thought perhaps it might be dogs running down a deer. The sound was far enough away that I could think such a thought without too much alarm. The dogs weren't feral or anything, I told myself, they were simply Rexes and Rovers that belonged to the local tobacco farmers, bored teen-aged pooches. Mind you, that sound grew nearer very quickly, and the imagined dogs grew more wolflike. Not only that, their numbers increased exponentially, and within a few moments the sound of barking filled the air. I recall thinking that at least my death would be fast, and perhaps even newsworthy: "Virtuous angler ripped apart by a thousand mad dogs." But what was ripped apart instead was the empty sky; it filled suddenly with geese, thousands of them, divided into hundreds of chevrons. These formations darkened the sky for a full minute or two before the last of the geese flew beyond the trees at the northern lip of the earth-bowl.

Spring, I said to myself, has sprung.

The reason I described that scene in some detail, the reason I remember it so clearly, is that it felt so like a reprieve. The hellhounds didn't get me. I don't simply mean the actual imaginary wild dogs, which I'd dropped to my knees to greet, offering my throat at a more accessible angle. That moment made me feel as if I'd avoided all manner of vicious hellhounds, and I tramped off towards the creek with whatever jauntiness I could muster in my waders.

It was the morning I became an angler. I happened upon a crook in the creek, a place where a felled tree and an irregularity in the land forced the little river to take a hard left. Across from me I could see the rounded elbow, and I noticed how the water had dug out earth from beneath the bank. I'm sure my eyes squinted cannily. *If I were a fish*, I suggested to myself, *I think I'd hang around right in there*. I lifted my spinning rod and flipped a tiny Mepps into the water. My cast came near enough the dark undercut to lure out the little rainbow. The fish came along willingly, being fairly smallish, perhaps ten inches. I also imagined that the fish knew I meant it no harm, that it was muttering along the lines of, "Yeah, yeah, very clever, buddy, you thought I'd be there and I was, blah-blah-blah." A single hook pierced the trout's lip. I slipped it out and gentled the fish back into the creek.

Then I turned around and marched back to bed, wanting nothing to mar my best day of fishing ever.

I did subsequently spend long hours beside the little river, learning—in a very slow, hit-or-miss fashion—about the nature of trout. I discovered that they didn't like the high heat of a summer's day, that you were likelier to encounter them as the sun rose or lay down. I learned the places where they liked to hide, under trees and felled logs, in the white water that splashed at the bottom of the weir. The creekside was heavy with brush, and in a few short weeks I'd developed a very idiosyncratic casting style, flipping out lures with a small, terse motion, as if the activity were secret and I didn't want people to catch me at it.

I got books out from the library in Port Hope. There was a section—a shelf or two—dedicated to angling. I simply started at the upper left and read them methodically. By the end of the summer I knew about fishing for dace in the River Tay. I knew how to take large-mouthed bass out of Okeechobee. I read books about tarpon-fishing, even though I had a strong hunch there were no tarpon in either the creek or the pond.

I read the patron saint of fisherfolk, Izaak Walton. I claim him for all anglers, even though snooty fly-fishers place proprietorial claims upon him, forming clubs and invoking his name, sitting around tying vises and turning large pieces of fluff—chicken ruff, marabou and peacock herl—into minute pieces of fluff. These are the men and women who sneer at bass fishermen, which I suppose is all right in the end, as these are the men and women whom bass fishermen slice in half with their outboard motors. But I think that few people have actually read Pa Walton's book *The Compleat Angler*, wherein he advocates angling with "a *worm* or any kind of *Flie*, as the *Ant-flie*, the *Flesh-flie*, or *Wall-flie*, or the *Dor* or *Beetle* (which you may find under a Cow-tird) ..."

An early favourite of mine was Zane Grey. At the turn of our century, Grey was, as we know, the most popular novelist in the western world, but his fame as an angler rivalled this, and was perhaps more widespread. He was known to the native peoples of all the continents, who had spotted the lean and haggard man trolling up and down in search of strange quarry. I've heard that Grey once trolled for a month. Not *went* trolling for a month, docking at eventide and going to bed, but trolling his *line* for a month.

Grey got my blood boiling—who could resist a book entitled *Tales of Fishing Virgin Seas?*—but it was a cheap rush, overwritten and overdramatic, and like any connoisseur (read *addict*) I soon developed more rarefied tastes. I became obsessed with fly-fishing. I read Roderick Haig-Brown, the judge who lived peaceably beside the Campbell River on Vancouver Island and wrote lovely books about his abiding passion. I read "Sparse Grey Hackle" and Lee Wulff. I discovered that some of my favourite authors of fiction had written about the sport: William Humphrey, Jim Harrison and Thomas McGuane.

One of the books I got out of the Port Hope Public Library was called *Fishin' Hats*. On the cover a young man raised a spectacular fish towards an old camera. The photographed colours were washed out and runny, but even so the fish was resplendent, wearing a brilliant coat of red speckled with little jewels.

The book was written in a homey manner and contained many stories about this fellow and his fishin' buddies (all of whom owned different hats, you see) and their various misadventures in various places. I cannot say with any honesty that it stood out amongst all the other books I was reading at the time. The writer seemed not as wise as, for example, Roderick Haig-Brown, and nowhere near as poetic. Haig-Brown doesn't go around dropping his *g*'s, for one thing, nor does he display a penchant for truly terrible practical jokes. One fact, however, was clear: the fellow who wrote *Fishin' Hats* may have been a better fisherman. Even discounting half of the book as lies and exaggerations, the author remained up there with the greats.

At summer's end, I moved back to Toronto and took up my existence as an impoverished writer of books and plays. Mostly in an attempt to fight off an all-consuming squalor, I asked for, and received from my friends, a fly outfit for Christmas. The rod seemed overly long to me. My favoured outfit of the day was a five-and-a-half-foot Ugly Stik, useful in torquing bass up from the shallows and propelling them into the boat with an emphatic *oomph*. So the fly reel possessed an eloquent simplicity. However, a small leaflet packed in its box proved baffling, full of strange instructions and commands. "How to Attach Backing to Fly Line," it read, whereupon there was a series of line drawings that appeared to represent worms performing the African Cluster Fuck. Even if I could have unravelled the pictographs, the leaflet failed to inform me just what exactly "backing" was. It's true that even a simple mind (which I lay claim to owning) could have figured it out. But even if I'd worked out "backing," there were any number of words that stopped me dead, much strange arcana. The nail knot, for example. Did they actually want me to go and get a nail in order to tie the knot? Yes, as things turned out, but that simple command was omitted. The magi who wrote the spells and charms simply assumed I held a nail in my hand at all times. And so I laid the new equipment aside and continued on with my super-torquing Ugly Stik, winching fishies up from down.

Now around this time in my life I was, as you may have gathered, immoderate in my leisure activities. My job as rock-and-roll musician placed me, from 9:00 P.M. until one in the morning, in various bars across the land. This was handy because that's where they seemed to keep all the beer and whiskey. After each gig we would thunder off to wind down, which we did by consuming amphetamines, washing them down with more beer and whiskey. Sometime around six in the morning we would pass out. Our sleep featured bad dreams and heart palpitations and was about as restful as a cattle drive. When we arose we would begin again.

This kind of lifestyle has repercussions on many levels. It takes its toll healthwise. I've paid most severely in the gums department. My gums are those of a seventy-year-old man. My periodontist says they are testament to years of ill health. Of course, worse than any physical debt is the one paid by your spirit. You end up with a tiny thing, perhaps the size of a postage stamp. A small and persistent pain is the only hint that it's there at all.

That is the situation I was in: weary in my being; excited, and at the same time confused, by angling literature. I was ready to meet my Old Guy.

A week after watching Gordon's casting display, the one where he sliced the banana held by his then-wife, I went back to the public school gymnasium with the fly rod I'd received for Christmas. The casters, three men and two teen-aged boys, were lined up along the centre red line, Hula-Hoops spread out around them. The casting was done in silence, the swish and whistle of fly line echoing off the varnished wood floor. Gordon hurried through this line as if the people were slalom pylons, pausing occasionally to watch a young fellow. He would grab a wrist, twist it so that the fly reel angled away from the torso. He would grab an elbow, wrest it away from a body. Sometimes, if he felt that the caster was allowing the rod to go too far forward, he would stand directly in front of him, nose pressed almost to nose.

Gordon saw me, hurried over and put the two pieces of my fly rod together. I truly don't remember him speaking to me, saying hello or whatnot, and I know that seems odd, but you should realize by now that the man is genuinely odd. Gordon assembled the fly rod, waved it in the air, gave forth a disdainful snort and tossed the rod aside. "Buggy whip," he said. I intuited that this was not good, although I was not sure why.

"Go get a club rod," he said, pointing towards the benches lining the gym walls, where there were several boxes of various shapes and sizes. I wandered over and found myself staring at a dizzying array of stuff. I didn't know enough about this specific fishing tackle to call it *junk*, but it certainly had the appearance of junk. I know enough now to tell you that it wasn't junk, exactly—all of the actual gear was fine and functional. But this stuff was mixed in with junk, tons of it, odds and ends that Gordon was pressing into service. There were numerous irregular patches of inner tubing, for example. These were used to straighten leaders. There was an endless variety of fluff, too, pieces that seemed too large to be mere lint, and of course they weren't. The fluff was to tie on the end of your fly line (once you'd straightened the leader with a piece of exploded tire) so that you could see it land in or around one of the Hula-Hoops (which, on closer examination, were bent and bandaged with masking tape). I managed to assemble a fly rod, I threaded the line through the guides, somehow I was canny enough to affix a pink dust-bunny to the end, and then I returned to the centre of the gym.

"All right," said Gordon, "let's see how you cast."

Those who haven't done it really have no concept that fly-casting is more complicated than waving the rod back and forth. I proceeded to do just that, quite pleased with myself. Gordon removed the rod from my hand. He was grinning at me oddly, warily, as though he thought me capable of advanced idiocy or violence. "No," he said simply, and for good or ill, I had found my Old Guy.

Gordon began to explain about fly-casting, how the idea was to decrease the size of the loop made by the fly line. He placed both hands around my wrist as though he could perform some sort of Vulcan Meld and thereby fuse my hand to the cork butt of my rod. He reminded me that the line must be allowed as much time behind and out of sight as in front. Then he disappeared.

I continued casting. Every so often Gordon would reappear, sometimes to re-perform the wrist lock, which didn't seem to take. He would come and stand directly in front of me, our noses almost touching, stopping me from bringing the rod so far forward, intoning that the cast is made between eleven and one o'clock on the hands of a huge imaginary timepiece. Gordon also—and I can't say I cared for this much—was wont to sneak up behind me and press his own knees into the back of mine, forcing me to buckle into a slight crouch. "Knees bent," he'd say, "the best way to perform any sort of athletic endeavour." Myself, I favoured a poncey attitude, my feet splayed regally, my free hand folded behind my back. But I couldn't begin to adopt this, because whenever I did, Gordon would sneak up on me and buckle me into the crouch. I might have gotten a little annoyed, except that Gordon would also turn up with a grin blossomed across his face. "Hey, hey, hey!" he'd say. "That's the way!" After a couple of hours, Gordon came and stilled my aching casting arm. "Now you've got it," he said. "Good work."

Gordon then demanded that all casters lay down the fly gear and take up the spinning equipment. I did so, believing that I might thereby reacquire some self-esteem, which I'd lost mostly up in the iron girders that formed the roof of the gymnasium, decorated now with brightly coloured lint balls. The club members used the whole length of the gym, standing behind the blue line at one end and throwing a plug at a target at the other. These targets consisted of a circle of plywood with a bright red fire alarm mounted in the middle.

A direct hit caused a satisfying and musical chime, not that I had any direct hits. My method of casting, which I felt had served me well, was apparently idiosyncratic and unexampled. Or, as the Old Guy put it, wrong. He had me pose with the rod in my hand, then repositioned my body roughly. "The first thing you do is move the rod tip *down*."

"Hmm?" You may well be brighter than I, but this direction seemed to make little sense.

"It's called loading the rod tip," said Gordon. "Here's your starting point." He held his hand out flat; I noticed that it trembled slightly. "First, down." The Old Guy folded his fingers. "Then up." He raised his fingers past the starting point, then levelled his hand emphatically. "Let the rod tip do all the work for you." I raised the rod like a fencing épée and did as the Old Guy had explained. I hit a fire alarm and produced a beautifully round *gong*. Mind you, the fire alarm wasn't on the target I was aiming at; still, I was very pleased.

I had practised and improved some over the years. There upon that magic isle, having assembled a rod and loaded it with a #3 Mepps, I was able to cast with great style and form. I went for distance, as there wasn't anything in particular to aim at, only the watery unknown.

Gary and Gordon had gone off scouting in the canoe, circling the island and looking for suitable camping spots. Paulo and I sat in the brush, nice and steamy, basking in sunshine. It seemed like a very nice island to me, although I hadn't really seen much of it beyond the shoulder-high bracken that encircled it. It reminded me of that fairy tale, *Sleeping Beauty*, the part where everyone and everything is slumbering, and the kingdom is strangled by gnarled ivy.

Had I been in a mood to worry about such things, it might have occurred to me that it was getting rather late in the day, that the sunlight was glancing off the water obliquely. But I wasn't in that mood, happy to be fishing where no one had ever fished before. I didn't know then that there was a good reason why no one had fished there before. I didn't even suspect this when my line started convulsing weakly and I brought to shore a tiny pike, which Paulo eyed with silence and disdain.

I tried hastily to release the fish, but the youngster had struck the lure voraciously and the lower set of treble hooks was embedded deep in its gullet. The pliers were somewhere in the mountain of luggage, which was now towering above us in the brush and tangle. Placing my finger in the pike's mouth I variously pushed, pulled and flicked the lure, but it was sincerely stuck. The fish died upon the table, so to speak, and with that my high spirits began to dissipate.

The canoe returned. "Well, the good news is," announced Gordon, "it looks fishy as hell. The bad news is, there doesn't seem to be anywhere to camp."

I thought that perhaps he was joking. I was admittedly a neophyte at such outdoorsy lore, but how could any piece of land not have someplace to camp?

"So here's our plan," said Gordon. "It's getting late. Gary and I are going to canoe over to that piece of land there"—he waved his hand across the water, very vaguely—"and see if there isn't anything better. But we might have to bivouac here for the night. Find temporary shelter and move the stuff across tomorrow."

Just peachy, thought I. We'd arrived only half an hour ago, and already we were seeking temporary shelter. How did the rest of it go? *Seek temporary shelter and essential foodstuffs, try to conserve bodily heat.*

Paulo also was not convinced that the island held no suitable camping spots. He set off on an inland exploration. Paulo didn't seem to notice or care that the island was buried under gnarly brush. He merely trampled across and through the vegetation, the three of us scrambling after him, accumulating lacerations on our hands and faces from the branches and thorns whipping in his wake.

And no less than fifty feet away from where our mountain of luggage rose there seemed, magically, to be a spot. Four trees grew in fairly symmetrical relation to each other, each marking one of the directions, making a square large enough—*just*—to contain the tent. (There was also a fifth tree, kind of a hanger-on, that stood just on the outskirts of this group like a skinny weird kid no one liked.) The ground was fairly regular, which, given the nature of the island, meant that there were no huge chasms or outcroppings.

As those three began to pitch camp, I was given the job of searching out a suitable place for the latrine. Gordon was quite specific about what was required, and I think to his mind, this location was even more crucial than the actual campsite. There had to be two trees growing shoulder to shoulder, so that stout branches could be nailed in a parallel fashion, and a toilet seat secured to them. A hole would be dug beneath. I found two likely trees, and I took spade in hand and began to dig. Except I did no digging at all. I merely ripped through the carpet of moss and peeled it back, and discovered the true nature of our new home. The island was really no more than a pile of stones, a huge cairn. Over time the rocks had been carpeted by moss. There was mois-ture and nutriment enough for some plant life to struggle upwards, skinny, crooked trees and plants with colourless flowers.

Other than this pitifully anemic flora there was no evidence of life. The four of us seemed to be in some forgotten episode of *Twilight Zone*, whereby while we were up in the Otter the universe was destroyed by a nuclear explosion.

Whilst setting up camp, Gary searched the trees and sky for a Canada jay. "You need a whiskey-jack in camp to bring you luck," he said to me. I looked up at the heavenly vault. Clouds scudded just above our heads, colliding like bumper cars. The world was birdless.

Gary also turned sharply to the left and squinted at distant furze. "Did you see something?" he asked me.

"No."

"I thought I saw something. Something white."

"No kidding?"

"They wouldn't have polar bears here, would they?"

"It's possible. Maybe the only things that survived were either up in airplanes or at one of the poles."

"Hmmm?"

"Just a theory."

Gary nodded, grabbed his hatchet, went to help set up camp. "I just thought I might have seen something," he muttered.

We made a couple of mistakes right from the get-go. For example, here's a very rough map of the island:

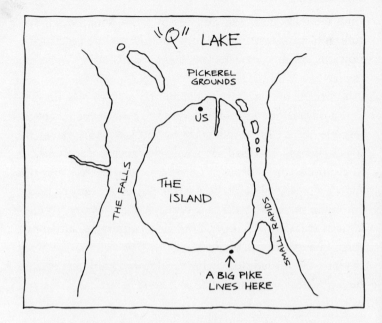

You'll notice that we're cleverly ensconced on the north shore there. Bad weather tends to come from the north and the east, which means that, essentially, we were laying naked our collective breast and shouting, "Come and get us!" But we could perhaps be excused for this: we *had* managed to locate the only suitable campsite on the entire island.

Having pitched the tent on the rectangle of ground formed by the four trees, Gordon instructed us to set up the kitchen, to make use of the various tarpaulins to provide shade and shelter. The kitchen consisted of a long bashed-up metal table. Gordon threw three wooden crates full of foodstuff on to it and then announced, "I had four boxes."

There was a brief interlude then, as we checked for an additional crate of food in the darkening furze. We didn't find it. (The search for this missing crate would occupy us, off and on, for the next few days, until it occurred to Gary that we didn't appear to be missing anything foodwise. At which point Gordon shrugged and said, "Maybe there were only three.")

Paulo tore apart some trees and strung up support beams. He lashed on the tarpaulins with strong cord and bungee cords, of which we had maybe four thousand. Gary stared at the gangly, nerdy fifth tree. "Maybe we should chop this down," he said sensibly.

Paulo, however, had already incorporated it into his construction, using it as an end to a crossbeam. This crossbeam had nailed to it vertically a shorter branch, at the end of which was a plastic cup. This held the tarpaulins up like a miniature big top. I will admit, Paulo's creation was not without a certain aesthetic appeal.

And so the tree remained. It even came to have a special use. Gordon approached it and drove a nail into its chest. He then deboxed a barometer and suspended it in our sight. The needle was lying, exhausted, to the most extreme left. This is not the side one wishes it to be on. We stared at it mournfully until Gordon recalled that a barometer has to be reset given the specific altitude, so he consulted maps and charts, played with a setting pin. The little needle quivered slightly and then lay back down again, obviously on its last legs.

We hung the barometer on the tree, consumed the most rudimentary of cheese sandwiches and climbed into our sleeping bags. Three of us slept in the tent. Gordon slept outside, his smiling face awash in starshine. He'd been proclaiming his intention of doing so for months. Every time he'd mentioned it, Gordon had snorted air through his nostrils lustily, as if the thought of rarefied Quebec air was so intoxicating that it actually improved the taste of the Toronto variety.

We listened to the low grumble of the rapids, the rapids wherein dwelt speckled trout of improbable size. We fell asleep dreaming of them.

I've yet to say much about the object of our quest. The Latin name is *Salvelinus fontinalis*, which translates, charmingly, as "a little salmon of the cold springs." I can also relate the following sort of thing: that the speckled trout isn't really a trout, it's a char. (Some people even spell that with two *r*'s, I'm not sure why, *charr*.) The most poetic name for the fish is the squaretail, which the species earned because the caudal fin is not indented.

If you pulled one out of the water—as the man did in Gordon's Super-8 movie "Broadback Memories"—it would take me a few seconds to realize what sort of fish it was. This is a startling admission, I realize, considering I'm the author of a book about fishing. One of the reasons for the candour is to illustrate how at odds the real world is with its bookish versions. As many times as you read about "the pectoral, ventral and anal fins running yellowish orange to scarlet," it doesn't prepare you for the astounding coloration of a wild brook trout. Especially during the spawning season, when fish wear the gaudiest sorts of coats in hopes of a good shagging. I would have to take a deep breath and ignore all the brightness; I would be forced to investigate more closely, to see if the speckles were indeed set in blue aureoles. I would look for the telltale vermicular design on the upper back.

That word, "vermicular," was first spoken to me by Gordon, my Old Guy, the occasion being a visit to his house in the wilds of Scarborough.

After a couple of months of attending the weekly meetings of the Scarborough Fly and Bait Casting Association, there'd been no real furthering of my relationship with the Old Guy. I would go to the gymnasium on Wednesday nights and practise fly- and bait-casting. My spirit was in repose and my knees were bent.

At night I would read my angling books and magazines, learning how to fly-fish for permit and grayling. My prospects of doing either—both required travel, to the south and north, respectively—seemed remote. These were not my salad days. I'd written one book, which had been ignored by critics and readers alike. I was not especially dispirited by this, and continued writing novels and plays in the early mornings, but most of the time I laboured in a bookstore, and my wages could not support even very modest dreams.

Then one day Gordon called and said he wanted to discuss my future with me. I was intrigued. Here I didn't know I had a future, and Gordon wanted to talk to me about it. Gordon gave me his address, and the next afternoon I hopped into my rusty Mustang and drove to Scarborough.

I suppose this warrants a comment or two, in case anyone out there is a little uncertain as to Scarborough's status. It aspires to citydom—has, indeed, a huge and slightly futuristic city hall, mushrooming in the middle of the Scarborough Town Centre, which is a shopping mall—but is in truth a suburban adjunct to Toronto. It abuts North York, another suburb that not only claims city status but proudly announces that it is the second largest one in Canada. I grew up in

North York, specifically that part called Don Mills. Victoria Park Avenue forms the boundary between Don Mills and Scarborough. The Don Mills side was mostly ravine; houses were built around the edges, imposing creations that put on airs of gentility. The planners gave these houses names like the "Don Briar," which I remember because that's what we lived in, the Don Briar, a construction that featured a fancy bricked façade and windows with ogee arches. The houses over in Scarborough were older and more humble, bungalows that sprouted across flatter, more barren land. Hydro towers marched through the neighbourhoods like creatures from an H. G. Wells novel. I don't wish to make general assertions such as, *The kids over in Scarborough tended to be mean and tough*, but I will say this: if you encountered a mean, tough kid, he or she was almost certainly from Scarborough. My high school, Victoria Park Secondary, lying on the border as it did, serviced both Don Mills and Scarborough. A further generalization: the Don Mills children were in the five-year academic program, while the kids from Scarborough were in the fatalistic four-year, concentrating on such useful occupations as shop, automobile mechanics and home economics.

So the Scarborough Fly and Bait Casting Association always had an odd kind of ring and feeling to it, as if guys with greasy hands and Export dead ends rolled up in their shirtsleeves were lined up streamside. I don't mean to sound like a snoot—hey, some of my best friends were from Scarborough—but I want to make a point of the resonance for me of Gordon's Scarborough connection.

Gordon's house, a small bungalow, lay on a crescent. It was surrounded by junk. To be fair, almost all of the junk was in the driveway, but such was its quantity and proximity to the domicile proper that it gave the impression of imminent besiegement. The driveway reminded me somehow of a slum in Calcutta. There were numerous constructions of corrugated tin: toolsheds, trash tins and lopsided barbecues. There were snowmobiles, some perhaps operational, but most patently the husks of dead snowmobiles. There were battered boats and a long flat thing, the shape of which suggested marine activity. There was a huge square trailer rendered out of plywood. It looked to be held together as much by the brake-light wiring as by any of the bolts and screws; the tires seemed pilfered from a lawn mower.

The small front lawn was occupied by an old maple tree. I mention that because, as junk-besieged as Gordon's residence looked then, in the middle of September, I would later discover it was nothing compared to the springtime, when Gordon would (a) tap the tree, suspending many buckets from the barky sides, and (b) use some of the corrugated tin constructions as boiling vats, the fires beneath sending up grey plumes of smoke.

I went to the front door and knocked lightly. Gordon appeared almost immediately, papers clenched in his little hand, reading glasses dangling, marmlike, across his breast. "Hello, Paul," he said. "Come in."

The inside of his house was much neater (at least the main floor was; I didn't know about the basement yet). One of the first things I saw, hanging on the wall of a small dining area, was a stuffed fish. There were many stuffed fish. Some sat in specially built boxes, behind sheets of glass, a style of taxidermy popular long ago. Others were fixed to plaques, their length and weight carefully etched onto accompanying squares of ornately bordered metal. Still more were posed with pieces of driftwood, and a few were eerily free-floating, the restless spirits of fish.

But one hulk caught and held my attention. "There's a big one," I noted.

"Eleven pounds," he said.

"What is it?" I asked.

"Hmmm?"

"What kind of fish is it?"

Gordon tilted his head, which he often does when puzzled by something I do or say. He turned and regarded the fish himself, as though a thief or some such miscreant might have snuck into the house during the night and pulled a crafty exchange. He turned back to me, his eyebrows knit with bafflement, and said, "That's a speckled trout."

"Oh, yeah."

Gordon used the stuffed fish as an instructional model. "Notice the spots," he lectured. "Notice the aureole. And see here." He lifted his finger and showed where the sides came together and rose up into the dorsal fin, spread by the taxidermist into an angry fan. "Notice the design here. It is vermicular."

I suppose it's not that startling a word, and easy enough to remember if you only try saying "worm" in a stagey German accent. Still, I was impressed.

"Let's go into the office," said Gordon, drawing me away from the creature.

In Gordon's little office there were more stuffed fish and countless photograph albums. They contained pictures of fish—Gordon and fish, to be sure, but also many other people with fish, some of whom I recognized as fellow club members. The photos also went back into history, turning black and white. They featured a younger Gordon, a cigarette dangling from his mouth. I realized I'd seen a photograph of this younger Gordon before: on the cover of that book *Fishin' Hats*.

Gordon placed his reading glasses upon his nose, but they seemed to interfere with, more than aid in, his reading. He twisted his neck, looking for a better angle, telescoping his arms in and out to find the proper focal distance.

"Now," he announced finally. "I think I understand your situation."

"Oh?"

"You're young, single. Not many worries or cares."

"I suppose."

"And if you were to die—"

"Hmm?"

"—you'd be buried and that would be the end of it."

"Well, yes, I guess so."

"But I don't want to talk to you about that."

"Okay. Good."

"That wouldn't be life insurance, would it? That would be *death* insurance."

This is the point where a dread and clammy realization set in.

"Would you say, Paul, that you could afford to pay fifty dollars a month?"

I paid four times that each month in bar tabs, so I nodded meekly.

"Excellent. Then let me show you this." This being the papers Gordon was clenching in his hands, which he now thrust under my nose. "I'm recommending to most of my clients that they take advantage of the plan set up by"...

some insurance company or another; it was too long ago and, truth be told, I've bought too many policies since then. Gordon always has some plan he's promoting, and over the years any change in my life—more money, marriage, the birth of children—has provoked a call about my future.

Fact: My Old Guy is an insurance salesman.

Corollary: I'm a seriously insured guy.

But I'm not such a dupe as you might suspect. That day, as Gordon prattled on and showed me how, at the age of sixty-five, I'd have several hundred thousand dollars to my name, my eyes narrowed cannily and I hatched a plan. I allowed him to complete the sales pitch, nodding occasionally as if I understood, and then when Gordon swooped in for the kill, placing papers in one hand and a cheap ball-point in the other, I said, "Take me fishing."

"What?"

"I'll sign these," I said, "on one condition. You have to take me fishing. Take me to one of your best places. A secret place."

I knew Gordon had secret places because whenever he reported great luck he would never answer the question, "Where were you fishing?", preferring to smile cryptically and change the subject.

Gordon checked his wristwatch. "We better hurry."

We raced down into the basement to gather up fishing gear.

Here's a question for anglers reading this modest tome: have you ever lost a rod tip? I know where it is: Gordon's basement. If you've misplaced the extra spool for your reel, it's there too. Gordon's basement is divided into two sections. One is the work area, at least, mixed in with all the broken and orphaned fishing tackle are mechanical contraptions. There are vices, for example, clamped to the corners of most of the tables. Being as the tables are o'erladen with stuff, the easiest way to locate one is to look for a vice. There are a couple of elaborate devices that resemble metal lobster traps —these are fishing-line reelers and dereelers usually bellied full with ancient monofilaments.

The other part of the basement is the leisure area, which is to say, if you could clear away some of the junk you'd locate sofas and chairs. The walls are adorned with Gordon's casting medals, dangling in dense clumps of gold, silver and brightly coloured ribbon. Fish are lined out across the walls, illustrating the history of taxidermy. The earliest mounts, trout killed when Gordon was a boy and a young man, are rigidly posed in tiny glass coffins, the background painted with crude representations of lakeland. The later catches are suspended on shellacked plaques, and their bodies are twisted, raging against the dying of the light.

We poked through the gear until we came up with two short rods and spinning reels. Then Gordon dove back after the tackle proper. This necessitated opening many plastic containers, all of which were secured by elastic bands. (I sometimes believe that Gordon feels elastic bands comprise the basic fabric of the universe.) In time he found what he was after, Mepps lures (#3s and #4s for them that cares).

Gordon donned his angling attire.

On the cover of his books (*Fishin' Hats* has a companion volume, *Fishin' Tales*) the young Gordon typically wore a corduroy shirt, flannel trousers and an Andy Capp cap. As he pulled on his fishing clothes that fall day, I saw that he hadn't changed his costume much in thirty-odd years. It dawned on me that he probably hadn't changed—or perhaps even *laundered*—the actual articles in question. They were, of course, patched and restitched, and although I couldn't tell for sure if that was the case, I wouldn't be surprised if his pant zipper was rigged up with elastic bands. Then he pulled on his fishing vest, made of material that would surely have disintegrated were it not bound together by junk, a tackle shop's worth, some of it suspended, like ornaments on a Christmas tree, by elastic bands.

We went to the driveway and shovelled out the car from beneath junk.

Outdoorsy folk usually have game and rugged vehicles, jeeps and other four-wheel drive conveyances. Gordon eschewed such things, opting instead for a great big American gas-guzzling land boat. He used this for the same purpose, i.e., going where ordinary cars ain't supposed to go. Many times since I've been startled as Gordon calmly turns the wheel to the right, piloting the steel whale into a farmer's field.

But I get ahead of myself in the telling. On the day I am relating, it merely seemed like a comfortable car, and I jumped in the passenger's side. Gordon assumed the driver's position, checked his rearview mirror and blind spot with exaggerated caution, and we were away.

We drove north, into the satellite communities that surround Toronto. I tried to remember the names of the towns—Goodwood, Woodbridge—and the turns we took. This was, after all, by way of being a *secret* fishing spot, and I understood, without its being said, that I would only be taken there once. If I couldn't find it again, by myself, then it was lost forever. But the mental directions I was compiling soon became overly complicated. The numbers of the concession roads jumbled together, the string of *right-left-left-right-left* became too random for memory to hold. Sometimes as the motorized frigate weighed down to a halt at a stop sign, Gordon would pull himself forward on the steering wheel and peer through the wind screen. He'd reach a decision and then whack at the steel bar that was the turn indicator, setting off a bomblike clicking that was silenced after we'd gone either right or left. I realized soon enough that I would never be able to find the secret place again. I realized—if not that day, then quickly enough—that I would never be able to do what Gordon was doing. We simply saw the land differently. I saw, and wanted to make sense of, a lopsided grid of pavement and dirt roads. I played dot-to-dot with the hamlets and burgs and tried to make a picture. Gordon was able to ignore all that, perhaps didn't truly apperceive it. He saw only the streams and rivers veined throughout the country.

This has its ugglesome side. Having driven to the stream he wished to fish, a riverlet so small that it could be stepped across at many points, Gordon parked the car and marched towards it. It seemed to be of no consequence to him that there was a big house in the way.

I personally am a meek and snivelling respecter of private property. "Doesn't somebody live there?" I asked.

"Oh, yeah," Gordon answered. "Nice fellow. And don't worry. The dog died."

"What dog?"

"He used to have this big dog. Barked a lot."

"But wouldn't bite?"

"Oh, sure. It was vicious."

We were at this time passing by the side of the house, entering the backyard, surely the domain of vicious dogs.

"Aren't you afraid he got a new dog?"

Gordon turned to me and grinned, which I counted for a senseless response at best. I think his point was that I worried too much, and it's true that there was no new dog at the house. Or he might have been grinning because he knew already that where we would strike out from the river, having fished a few hundred yards of it, there would be a dog that hadn't died.

We walked through the backyard, through the shrubbery, and neared the little creek. Gordon made his approach very stealthily indeed, virtually on tiptoe. Still some feet away, Gordon stopped abruptly, flipped the back of his hand so that he smote me upon the breast, and began to make peculiar and frantic gesticulations. It took a long moment to interpret them, but I finally cottoned on. The bank was undercut on the far side, that was what the scooping motion signified, and I was to try a pendulum cast, hence the tick-tocking motion. I squeezed through the foliage—Gordon's urgent hushing sounds filling the air—until I had a clear shot at the creek.

At the weekly club meetings, Gordon had introduced me to a spin-casting game called Arenberg, popular in Europe, not played so much here in North America. Arenberg demands that you make the casts with diverse deliveries—side-arm, underhanded, cross-body. I was fairly adept at this because of my idiosyncratic learning on the stream upon my father's land.

There was a complication, however, an oddity to the actual spinning equipment. The reel lacked a bail, the metallic arch that covers the face and corrals monofilament. One usually flips this back with the non-casting hand, allowing the line to fly away unhindered, and then re-engages it with a jerky snap of the cranking handle. Gordon had sawed the bail off the reel I was using, leaving behind just a small tooled and grooved metallic stub. He instructed me to lift the line free with my right forefinger, cast and then pick it up with this same digit, slipping the line into the pickup.

The reason for this is so that the lure can be engaged as soon as it strikes the water, so that there aren't long moments of fumbling with the bail while the bait sinks to the bottom to search out dead branches and sharp rocks.

My forefinger did not appear to be up to this manoeuvre, being, in keeping with the rest of my body, short and squat. The secret, Gordon informed me, is to raise the rod tip, which brings the line and forefinger closer together. It's a matter of simple physics. I don't understand the physics, but that's what it is.

So I thrust my little rod in the direction of the undercut, allowed the line to drop until the Mepps dangled near the top of the water. I swung the lure back and forth and lobbed it—somewhat deftly, I have to say, because it's very possible to fluke into the realm of deftness—towards the far bank. Just before the lure hit I lifted the rod and stuck out my index finger. The line dutifully came home to rest. The Mepps hit and I made it frolic momentarily in the current. A small rainbow trout darted out from its lair and took it.

I removed the hooks from the fish's mouth as gently as possible. When I turned around Gordon was grinning maniacally and holding his right hand high in the air. I tilted my head quizzically, wondering what he was up to. He gave every indication of being about to strike me.

"Come on, man," he said, his raised hand wiggling a bit.

"What?"

"*Come on.*" The words had to sneak past his maniacal grin, which Gordon was unwilling or unable to abandon.

"What?"

As if speaking its name would ruin the magic, Gordon performed the ritual as best he could, striking down emphatically at where my hand should have been, had I offered it forward to be slapped. I then obediently proferred my upturned palm, but the moment was gone.

"Do you want that fish?" asked Gordon. "That's a good size to eat. Fits in the fry pan nicely."

"Oh! That's a good idea."

Gordon took the fish and broke its neck. He produced a knife from somewhere on his clanky junk-festooned person and slit the creature's belly, sliced through just behind the head and pulled. The offal came away with the head, which he tossed aside. He then stuck his thumb into the cavity, running his thick nail down the length of the backbone, extruding a gob of bloody mucus. Gordon picked up some vegetation from beside the creek, stuffed into the fish's new belly cavity and stowed the cleaned fish away.

We worked our way upstream. As we approached the next spot, Gordon would describe what we would find. "This is good," he might say. "There's a big log in the water up here."

"Oh, good."

"It's a little tricky, though."

By "tricky," Gordon typically meant that you couldn't get near the big log for all the tangled gnarls and brush. Or that the big log lay behind a complex arrangement of smaller logs. Sometimes trees pushed limbs across the breadth of the rill, as low and tortuous as limbo poles. Gordon would always offer me first crack at these places; I would decline. He would shrug, step forward and make the cast. He almost always made them successfully, and should the cast be ill-aimed or short, Gordon would abort the mission midair, jerking the rod so that the Mepps came screaming back at us without ever having touched water. "You only get," Gordon explained to me, "one chance."

That first day of fishing has melted down in my mind somewhat, and to tell the truth, I have difficulty separating it from other fishing trips I made with my Old Guy. What I'm doing now, in writing about it, is picturing the size of the river, for that is the easiest way to differentiate. We fished this creek—which Gordon long ago christened "Itsy-bitsy"— fairly rarely, so the memories I have are likely to come from that first trip.

If they don't, who cares?

This one surely does. Gordon took a step to be close to the creek. He then keeled over backwards, his hand tearing at the fishing vest right where his heart would be. Gordon landed in a nearby copse and sat there, eyes glazed, breathing heavily. His mouth moved rapidly, but no words came out.

"What's the matter?" I asked gently, foolish words to be asking a fellow clearly in the throes of a death rattle.

"Abra ... abra ... abra ...," Gordon stammered. "A brown trout."

"Brown trout?"

Gordon held up trembling hands and measured a distance of about a foot and a half. "Brown trout," he whispered. "Didn't you see it?"

This is a familiar refrain between Gordon and me. *Didn't you see it?* No. No, I didn't see it. A porky brown trout had been startled out of its hole, it had petulantly darted away down the length of Itsy-bitsy, likely throwing up a rooster tail, and I had failed to notice. I don't know if this is because I am usually wrapped up in my own problems or if I'm congenitally dull and unobservant. I don't know if there's any difference between the two.

We awoke that first morning on our island to the howling voice of Murphy.

You are no doubt all familiar with the popular fictitious philosopher Murphy, whose First Law states that when something can go wrong, it will.

What could have gone wrong—and therefore did—was that the wind picked up.

It came at us with an insistence that bordered on ferocity. It flapped all the canvas of the tent and demanded to be let inside. It shook the trees until they lost their few pallid leaves. It stirred up the water until the lake was doing a passable imitation of Honolulu, white foamy water beating against the shoreline, ferrying decaying animal and plant matter until our campsite was surrounded by a fetid roiling reef.

Occasionally, very occasionally, the wind would die suddenly and leave behind a silence, empty and eerie enough that one or the other of us would remark, "Looks like the wind's dying down." Immediately the wind would return with renewed vigour, sharper and colder then before, having just nipped off to the North Pole for a refreshing puff of snappy arctic air. Gordon was the first to notice this trend, and when Paulo opened his mouth to remark on one of these disquieting quells, Gordon hushed him frantically.

"Don't say the word," said Gordon.

"Which word is that, Gordon?"

"You know. The word."

"Wind?"

The wind made an interesting re-entrance; it had become, technically, a *simoom*, having managed to scrape up some dirt from somewhere. It blasted this into our eyes and then disappeared for more.

"Yes, Paulo. That word."

"All right, Gordon, I will not say 'wind.'"

The wind now leapt into the campsite with the energy of a troika dancer, destroying one of the structure's crossbeams. Paulo flew into action, tearing another small tree out of the ground and laying it alongside the broken beam, lashing the two together with nylon and bungee cords.

"All right, Gordon, I will not say this word. But what shall I say?"

Gary suggested "Murphy," redolent of the grim ministrations of the Fates. This was soon commonly accepted, although we tended to simply call the wind "Murph." We were certainly on familiar terms. Murph knew us intimately, routinely finding any holes in our underwear and seeing how small he could render our privates with his frigid fingers.

Every so often one or the other of us would misspeak himself. Paulo, the most optimistic, was ever vigilant of changes in the weather. He would take down the barometer and tap it with his huge forefinger, usually provoking the needle to rise halfheartedly and virtually imperceptibly. "Look!" Paulo would exclaim, like a child on Christmas morning who's just unwrapped a Lamborghini. "Oh, my." Then Paulo would present his broad face to the north and if, when he turned away, he still had his moustache, Paulo was likely to assert, "And I'm not kidding you, the wind is dying down."

The three of us would groan as Murph raged into the camp like a whirling dervish, having upgraded himself for a bit to cyclone status. He toppled the vertical stays and the tarpaulins, deposited his load of water down the back of our shirts.

Using the "w" word (you can see that I'm still reluctant to do so, thousands of kilometres away, warm and dry in the house which, like the wisest of the three pigs, I have built out of brick) came to be known as "tempting Murphy." I rapidly extended this usage so that it applied to other things. Most other things. Going near the canoe was tempting Murphy, because Murph would immediately show us some nice rollers he'd been saving, waves that came from all directions and covered the water with foamy tumult. Going to the john was tempting Murphy. He would not only bring along a fresh load of polar air, he would take the toilet paper out of your hand and fling it into the soggy brush twelve feet away.

(Mind you, I had additional problems in this regard. My visits to the crude latrine were taken as a personal insult by the only other living creature on the island, a demented squirrel that had survived nuclear annihilation because no one, even God, gave a rat-shit about him. As soon as I sat down he would appear three feet above me on one of the trees, aimed in my direction, baring sharp teeth and making a series of harsh kecking sounds. This did bring the benefit of hasty evacuation. Gordon suffered oppositely. On the first day he visited the latrine out of duty, came back and reported with a shrug that there was not much doing in that regard. This was still happening on the fourth day, although his shrugs had become much less insouciant. By the sixth night Gordon was panicked and groaning; he picked listlessly at his dinner and wondered if his life were in danger.)

The point I was getting to, before that last bracketed and somewhat distasteful paragraph, was that the very act of going fishing was therefore tempting Murphy. But fishing we went, that first morning, with Murph fluffing our hip waders. We chose to begin our explorations on the east side of the island, at the set of smaller rapids.

Paulo and Gary set off in the canoe, not using the antique engine because very occasionally Murph could be helpful, and that was one favour he'd do you, he'd blow you around the top of the island to the small rapids at a second's notice. Of course, he'd do this also when you wanted to go elsewhere. Gordon and I went in the collapsible boat, an invention I think may work well in practice, although not in theory.

Gordon and I parked the collapsible boat—invented, you may recall, by Nero, in one of his more creative attempts to murder his mother—on the west side of the rapids, snugging it in against a bank of furze. Paulo and Gary propelled the canoe across to the other side where it found harbour in the lee of a large rock. There were numerous large rocks popping out of the water, boulders of Wagnerian stature. The water bubbled around them, and as we climbed out of our vessels, the cloud cover broke and sunlight smacked the scene.

Gordon found shallowness and purchase enough to wade out upon the water with his fly rod. The trees and brush behind were very dense, so Gordon covered the water with a roll cast. He seemed to do this effortlessly, despite Murph's interference. I moved upriver on Gordon and commenced tossing tin, which is to say, I had my spinning gear and was trying to hoodwink brookies with a #3 Mepps. Across the rapids, Paulo and Gary were doing the same. Gary worked his rod with seasoned ease; Paulo possessed more flair, favouring a pendulum cast, snapping a long length of line in a circle before propelling it towards the white water. And I was not doing too badly myself, especially in the aim department. My time spent crouched ("the best position for any athletic endeavour") and huddled with Gordon on tiny creeks was paying off on the bigger water. I'd spy the undercut and direct my Mepps unerringly towards it, dropping it neatly before any trout that might be wondering about its next meal. To put it bluntly, we might not have been fishing too good, but we were casting like nobody's business.

The distinction that I just made is not quite as dumb as it sounds, because I've actually met casters who have never caught a fish. And there are a number of casters who don't enjoy angling; although they may do it from time to time, they much prefer tossing plugs across an empty field, setting hookless flies upon pool or pond. These are tournament casters, a rare breed indeed.

The history of the sport is a little vague. The first known tournament took place in Central Park, in the year 1864. It was based on a challenge issued by Seth Green to Reuben Wood. (Seth Green actually comes into our story in a couple of ways, for he was the man who first constructed hatcheries and began rearing speckled trout, helping the species to propagate and multiply.) The first national tournament was held under the auspices of the National Association of Scientific Angling Clubs and was held in Racine, Wisconsin. That governing body became the National Association of Angling and Casting Clubs and is now the (far more eloquent) American Casting Association. There is a chapter in Toronto, and Gordon was for many years an active member. But he had difficulties with some of the other casters, to the extent that he quit the sport in 1957 and didn't take it up again until 1974.

Gordon's casting career is pretty remarkable: he has held over sixty records, both nationally and internationally. He has been the North American All-Round Senior Champion nine times.

And here you probably didn't even know that the sport existed.

There are twelve different competitions. Many casters excel at one or two, but the idea is to compete in them all. And the world's best tournament casters—the American Steve Rajeff, his countryman Rene Gillibert, the Norwegian Oyvind Forland, the German Wolfgang Feige—are the world's best at each and every event.

Half of the events relate to bait-casting, half to fly. They are further subdivided into distance and accuracy contests. The accuracy events seem the most straightforward. The venue is usually a manmade pool or cultivated pond. Five targets—in the form of slightly oversized Hula-Hoops, thirty inches in diameter—are configured upon the water, the closest and farthest according to specified parameters; the other three (or four, in the game called Bass Bug) placed randomly in the intervening space.

The bait-casting subdivisions are made by weight: ¼ oz., ⅜ oz., ⅝ oz. The heavier plugs are thrown with bait-casting equipment, those barrel-shaped reels that one must thumb. Otherwise casters tend to use spinning gear. The fly accuracy events are Bass Bug, Dry Fly and Trout Fly, a dainty hybrid that requires the caster to kneel and make a third round of roll casts. The procedure is fairly straightforward. One starts with the nearest target. The caster can false-cast as many times as he or she likes, assessing the distance, and then the fly is set down. There is, wouldn't you know, a judge standing in the water. If the fly falls within the ring or on its rim, he clenches a fist and shows this to the scorekeeper: *perfect*. He awards a demerit point per foot away from the ring. This is not a precise science; no measurements are taken. At any rate, if the question is whether the fly was three or four feet away, it's kind of a moot point as far as the standings are concerned. Because the trick here is to make no mistakes whatsoever, to throw the round clean. Ticks (accidental strikings of the water's surface), too many false casts during certain phases of the game, illegal strips and laydowns earn demerit points.

The Bass Bug, which is played with a tiny cork attached to the line, adds a wrinkle to the other games: there is an additional target set up in the pool, sixty-five to seventy feet farther away. This distance must be achieved by using the good old Double Haul.

But the fun comes in the distance games. The three fly games are Angler's Fly, Single-Handed Salmon and Double-Handed Salmon. Angler's Fly is played with a shortish section of fly line, a shooting head. The competitor lays out running line, monofilament, in a configuration upon the ground, a series of overlapping figure eights, and then lifts the heavier fly line into the air. Whereas the Double Haul employed in the Bass Bug is a subtle action, the left hand tugging oppositely in a quick, short motion, in the Angler's Fly the action is emphatic and grand. The second haul sometimes has the magnitude of a discus hurl or something, and casters come up with an odd assortment of grunts and spewings. I was once exhorted by a fellow caster to make my haul with "vigour and conviction," words I try to live by. On the same occasion, I remember, Gordon spotted something wrong with my technique and pointed out that this vigorous second haul should be made at the precise moment that my wrist broke. Imagine the right hand pulling the rod through the air; the wrist must snap, overturn like a baseball batter's. Once I had those ideas firmly in place I was able to execute this cast with a beauty and perfection that still leaves me breathless. *Once.* And, I believe I mentioned, I was standing on my running line, so the cast went absolutely nowhere. I relate this story—twice, now—because it cuts to the heart of casting. The distance is but the most tangible measurement. The art and joy lie elsewhere, in the harnessing and releasing of energy, in the *timing*, yes, but in an even more precise sense of that word, in feeling right at home in a single instant.

From the Angler's Fly the equipment gets bigger. In Double-Handed Salmon the competitors stumble out onto the field supporting *telephone poles* in their hands, for heaven's sake, seventeen-foot rods that they work with vigour and conviction. There are places on the globe where these rods are actually used—Scotland, for example, the land that invented the caber toss.

The bait-casting distance games feature very peculiar equipment. The unrestricted ⅝-oz. revolving spool event uses short, thick rods and tiny reels. The line is so light that twenty-eight miles of it weigh only an ounce, hence the game's nickname, the Spiderweb.

The reel used in the two-handed spinning event is oddly shaped, the main body of line held on a spool, but much of it wrapped around a conelike appendage to the reel face. This is my favourite event to watch. The caster stands within a circle holding the rod before him, his legs bent, usually one toe delicately placed to the ground. He looks like nothing so much as a samurai warrior. With much concentration the competitor begins to swing the lure. He builds up potential energy and then allows the weight to complete a circle around his head. The lure is thrown; every part of the caster is incorporated into the motion, every ounce of force lent to the cast.

Gordon's personal best in this event is 564 feet, which falls just 10 feet shy of the world record.

There isn't, as far as I know, a Tournament Casters' Hall of Fame. If there were, it would house busts of men like Pierre Creusevaut and Jon "Buddy" Tarantino. Tarantino is the most famous of them all, a handsome young man who, I've been told, once graced the cover of *Sports Illustrated*. Tarantino was gunned down during a robbery at the family grocery store. The Tournament Casters' Hall of Fame would have statues and plaques for men like Charles Ritz—the theoretician of the Double Haul—and Myron Gregory, who developed the weight-forward line that made the Double Haul possible.

There would be a bust of Gordon.

But, I'd have to say, the Tournament Casters' Hall of Fame would be in a pretty small building. Hell, it would be a *room* in a small building. There simply have never been a lot of people competing at the sport, and for this reason a neophyte caster soon encounters those who are tilting for global domination.

This is how I ended up in Cincinnatti, entered in the North American championships.

I'll tell you my results, mostly because there are no doubt still records extant—the American Casting Association is nothing if not scrupulous in its record-keeping—and I don't want to be uncovered as a liar. I will therefore confess that my best result, in any game, indicated a kind of low-grade mediocrity. My worst came in the ⅝, the heaviest plug. It was pouring rain, so I cast with a draping of protective yellow plastic, which interfered with all my movements, which were not necessarily the most appropriate movements to begin with. I remember a kind of stunned silence from the spectators as I cast. The judge waded around the water with all of his fingers extended in a friendly "Hey there!" fashion. Very occasionally he would collapse a digit, indicating a cast that he charitably deemed to be within nine feet of the plastic hoop. Then the finger would pop up again. I'm just glad he didn't have more fingers, because he could have made much use of them.

So it was a dismal tournament from that point of view, at least for me. Gordon, competing with the older casters, won quite a few games and the overall Master's championship. Once again, Gordon was the best Old Guy in North America. One of our club members was the second best kid in North America. Steve Rajeff was the absolute best in North America. I was the worst, but there's no point harping on that.

It has since occurred to me that a lot of what my Old Guy does is a kind of railing against the notion that any human being is a puny, insignificant thing. As soon as you pick up a fly rod he will be at your side, holding your wrist to keep it locked and whispering in your ear that if you learn what he has to teach, you could be the best: in North America, in the world. He's told this to people with far less talent than even I. Gordon has told this to people with imperfect control over their limbs, people whose every motion is a hardship. *Learn from me,* he tells them, *and you can be the best in the world.*

That attitude informed our trip to the northern Quebec extreme, as well. *I am here for a specific purpose,* Gordon had told Richard Demers, namely, to catch the biggest speckled trout *in the world.*

Because whatever God is out there, Gordon seemed to be saying, *had best not underestimate me.*

Gary took a respectable speckled trout out of the rapids, a couple of pounds' worth. He took it on spinning tackle, lacking the advanced skill that would allow him to roll-cast into the ugly face of Murphy whilst backed up against the furze. Gordon managed to take but one fish, a brook trout of perhaps eight inches. This wasn't a very good day's fishing, but it seemed somehow acceptable. There were fish in the neighbourhood and we had every confidence that the next dawn would bring out the big boys, lusty eight- and nine-pounders, perhaps the fish that would retire Dr. Cook's dusty squaretail.

So back to the camp we went. Murphy had done a little damage, blowing out one of Paulo's wooden fundamentals, tilting a puncheon. Paulo effected repairs, lashing supporting beams to the existing structure with nylon cord—of which, you may recall from the packing list, we had two hundred feet—and bungee cords. While he worked at this, Gary retired to the tent, took out his journal and began writing quietly. I sat outside but nearby, smoking a cigar; I spoke to Gary often, making small and insignificant comments, not for the sake of conversation so much as to distract Gary from this scribal activity. I myself had not made one solitary note; I couldn't even think of a note as an abstraction.

Leonidas Hubbard, the man from *Outing* magazine who set out to make his reputation by traversing Labrador, was a great one for making notes. At the end of every long day he would sit and labour quietly, detailing the particulars:

First snow came, mixed with nasty cold rain. My trousers hanging in strips and tatters. My moccasins showing sock at most every angle ...

Now, I would be remiss in my duties as official trip scribe (which I will continue to consider myself until Gary publishes whatever he was scribbling down in his journal) if I did not mention, however briefly, Gordon's skill as a cook. What he rendered out of the fish we had caught that day was *filets amandines*. This was accompanied by potatoes au gratin and glazed carrots. Gordon had supplied us with a menu some months prior to our departure, although—typically—it got left behind. Still, many of the meals were repeated or approximated, and if I note a few selections here, it might demonstrate the kind of thing we got, and got used to.

Monday's dinner, for example—although how quickly we lost the notion of a "Monday"—was supposed to be:

Poached brookies with parsley-lemon cream sauce served with wild rice pilaf, Caesar salad and French stick.

What scuppered that supper was a dearth of brookies. How about:

Baked pickerel stuffed with wild rice, celery and onions, creamed parsley carrots and white rice. Dirty-brown puddin' cake, tea or milk.

Now *that* one we actually ate. Yummy.

Paulo and I had been given the assignment of catching four pickerel of a certain size, namely, the correct size for the Coleman oven, which is basically a square metal box outfitted with a series of internal racks that don't quite fit. The heating source is the Coleman stove, an oblong box with (in our case) three burners. Only the centre burner provided a healthy and tractable flame—the other two, adjunctive, were weaker and much more likely to get blown out by Murphy. The Coleman stove required much care and attention. Gordon was constantly leaping over to it, drawing out the plunging device from the fuel tank, priming the cooking flame into blueness. They are not the easiest contraptions in the world to operate. Gary told a joke about a neophyte parachutist who leapt from the plane and became confused as to which cord to pull. As the parachutist plummeted towards the ground he encountered a man headed in the opposite direction. "Know anything about parachutes?" he asked. The man shook his head. "Sorry. Know anything about Coleman stoves?"

The most troublesome thing, however, was logistics. Pots would have to be balanced one on top of the other, the topmost serving as a heating unit only, the pot in the middle steaming vegetables, the bottom bubbling with cooking fury. Gordon never evidenced any great concern that things might go awry. He checked his pots quite often, lifting off a lid (usually dropping it to the ground with a cry of great pain) and peeking inside. "Four minutes," he might adjudge calmly. He'd stir a sauce, place his hand on top of the Coleman oven to judge its current efficacy (usually crying out in great pain, sticking his fingers into his mouth) and tell Paulo to get the plates. Paulo was, invariably, in the midst of adjusting the wooden superstructure. But plates were got and handed out, and the meal was served.

I broke several land-speed consumption records. My personal best was—well, actually I don't know, I was too busy eating to time myself. The reasons for the speed are evident. For one thing, Murphy could cool off a plateful in just a few seconds, reduce it all to frigid gluten. For another, I was always hungry. Dinner came after several hours of activity. Fishing might not seem arduous, and I am always slightly embarrassed when I aver that it is, feeling like one of those grog-puffed pub dwellers who maintains that walking to and from the dart board constitutes exercise. Arm-flailing aside, consider perambulation whilst standing in a river of some considerable force. Consider getting to the water, which we accomplished either over land, hiking through the dense brush in our waders and rain gear, or by water, in which case we paddled in a frenzied ebullition, trying to overcome Murphy.

But, some of you keener readers might be asking, didn't you mention an outboard motor? Oh, that's right, I did, and it looked for a while as though that ancient piece of machinery might prove our salvation. However, on that first day of fishing, we judged Murphy's ferment and decided that the collapsible boat was unworthy. It was, after all, a galvanized scow, squarish and difficult to manoeuvre. So we sheltered it out of the wind, tied it to a piece of sturdy furze and hoped it would outlast Murphy's wrath. The four of us climbed into the War Canoe. Gordon pulled a length of hemp and the antique motor coughed and choked. In this manner we moved confidently around the island, back to our campsite.

It was somehow left to me to deal with the canoe. Not a task I was unwilling to do, you understand, but I may have been the worst candidate for the job. Being a bear of very little brain, I feared—unreasonably—that the canoe would somehow get stolen from its moorings and washed out to sea. How this was going to happen in the face of Murphy's relentless pounding remains a mystery of compelling depth. But, as I had been taught to do on little canoe trips over Ontario's friendly cottage-dotted water, I hauled the bow out of the water and set it up on high ground. I then wiped my hands, satisfied with a job well done, and went to eat.

Sometime during the night, the weather turned bad on us. It had previously been merely awful, Murphy petulant and cranky. He now turned nasty, flapping the canvas of our tent, ripping out the uprights and crossbeams of our crude scaffolding. It had rained briefly, "briefly" only because the rain almost immediately became snow and ice pellets.

Sometime in the middle of that cruel night Gordon spread the tent flaps and stood there shivering. He clutched his sleeping bag about him like a beggar's rags, although it was now rain-bloated and probably weighed hundreds of pounds. Gordon could control his trembling lips only enough to let thick, unintelligible profanities tumble out.

The tent was already crowded—Paulo occupied half of it, or so it always seemed, and his socks took up the rest—but we could hardly turn the Old Guy away.

We made room inside the tent.

I awoke at dawn. Which is to say, light was halfheartedly spattering the darkness, so I assumed it was dawn, although the day was to get no brighter. I guess some portion of my brain had been thinking through this canoe business while I slumbered. Or perhaps I was unconsciously alerted by the absence of a certain sound, namely, that of a canoe being beaten up against rock. For whatever reason, I rose groggily, pulled on several articles of clothing—a few shirts, a couple of pairs of pants—and stuck my head through the tent flap.

My cheeks ruffed and fluttered like the canvas, until the sleet hardened and they turned gelid. I was sticking my face into the most gruesome weather. It came from the North Pole, which seemed none too distant at that moment, just behind the bank of bloated, hoary clouds. I hurried down to the water and saw just how heartless Murphy could be.

He'd drowned the ancient Johnson outboard motor.

Too late I realized that if I hadn't pulled the bow so far out of the water, Murphy would not have been able to commit this murder. But I had, and it was easy for him to flick the stern over sideways and submerge the engine. The cowling had become detached and bobbed up against the shoreline. The gas tank floated a few feet away, connected by its rubber umbilical.

I climbed into my waders and dealt with the situation as best I could, bailing out the boat and reassembling the motor parts. The other fellows had not risen, and I glumly climbed back into my sleeping bag, not even bothering to remove my wet clothing. I pulled my Walkman out from my travelling bag. Affixing the earphones over my frozen flaps, I selected, to combat the oncoming depression, Beethoven's Seventh Symphony. Even that didn't seem to help. I flicked off the machine—I left the earphones on, savouring the small but precious foam-rubber warmth—and went back to sleep.

Since I had become one of his intimates—having fished with him and purchased insurance—Gordon elevated my status in the Scarborough Fly and Bait Casting Association. The club had no offical stations, as such, although Gordon was clearly president. And now that I think of it, there was a fellow named Rod, a friendly, quiet schoolteacher, whom Gordon had made treasurer owing to Rod's ability to not make arithmatical mistakes. Beyond that, there were no rankings; however, I think I became sergeant at arms or something along those lines. My duties included things like arriving early at the school gym on Wednesday nights, setting up the targets, assembling a number of fly and spinning rods. By this time I was improved enough in my own casting that I was allowed (even encouraged) to stop beside those more inexperienced than I to gently point out weaknesses. From time to time I would even stand directly in front of a new caster, staring that person in the eye and showing him or her how the rod need never go farther than one o'clock on the huge imaginary clock so beloved of casters.

The club numbered perhaps twenty-five at its healthiest. It was composed of people like Rod, the treasurer, quiet and sobersided, and Paul, a loud, portly sort who was very talkative, which wouldn't have mattered too much except that he had a pronounced stutter. He was not in the least shy about it, which is good, but he also thought nothing of leaving listeners waiting up to a minute for the next syllable to emerge from his mouth. One time another club member, Ben, suggested helpfully (and seriously), "How about if every time you get stuck I give you a smack on the back of the head?" Benny was a Scarborough boy. He drove a car with retro-blasters, or some such thing, rising out of the hood like a pipe organ from a vaudeville stage. There was a teen-aged boy named Brad, quiet and studious, and his friend Steve, who dressed exclusively in Megadeth T-shirts. There was Janet, a large woman who came to the club not so much to cast as to complain bitterly of the treatment she was accorded at the hospital in which she worked. These were the ones I remember as being most regular, back in those first days of my involvement with the club.

On some summer evenings we would practise in a huge field with the strange equipment, some outfits tiny, others ludicrously long. Other evenings the club would assemble at Scarborough's city hall complex, where there was a long, square outside pool. It had no doubt been designed for purely aesthetic reasons—no one could swim in it; it was shallow and wrought of scrapey concrete—but Gordon was able to make use of it, donning his hip waders, climbing in and distributing Hula-Hoops. We played the various games: Dry Fly, Trout Fly, Bass Bug. Bass Bug's sixth target mostly seemed distant and unattainable, but occasionally, when I hit the Double Haul correctly, the piece of cork would float down in that target's vicinity. This felt good. Once or twice the bug landed within the ring of plastic, and then Gordon, standing in the water and acting as judge, would clench his fist and shake it in the air, once, with emphasis. I find it interesting that this action has acquired general popularity—think of all the sitcoms where it has become a guaranteed laugh, a character punching the air with a balled fist and exclaiming "Yes!"—because it is only within the rare realm of tournament casting that it has specific and eloquent meaning—*perfect, no demerits.*

At the end of that first summer—after my elementary education and subsequent humiliation in Cincinnatti; after the first two-man sorties into the valleys of southern Ontario—Gordon announced to the club that it was time for a club fishing trip.

We went to the town of Southampton, on the Saugeen River, which flows into Georgian Bay. In the fall, salmon begin to move upstream, hoping to complete their life cycle in their very place of creation. These fish are not the quarry; they are autodigesting, their fins shrinking and blanching, the rest of their bodies turning a diseased black, crosshatched with scars and scratches.

What one fishes for, autumn days on the Saugeen, are rainbow trout. These are anadromous rainbows, which leave the comfy quarters of their home streams and journey out to Georgian Bay, where they grow large in the big water. It is a matter of some small controversy whether or not these fish are technically "steelhead"—the appellation given to the West Coast rainbows that seek yearly adventure in the ocean—but we often call them that. (I don't suppose they are; a true steelhead would have to smolt, i.e., undergo a physical change allowing it to breathe the salt water. Our steelheads can be, however, as big as their West Coast brethren—twenty pounds, often—and might be more fun to catch, given the relative sizes of the rivers and streams out of which they're taken.) The idea behind the angling is: the black salmon come up to spawn and die, and in their wake come the lively silver-sided steelhead, gobbling up salmon roe.

The usual bait presentation, therefore, is a small and eloquent representation of a salmon egg. These can be rendered out of foam rubber, or regular rubber, or yarn. You can also fish with salmon eggs, placing anywhere from one to four inside a little square of gaudily coloured netting and tying up this little bundle with thread. We spent the night prior to our angling making such bait, fourteen fellows booked into a single motel room, Janet occupying the room next door. Gordon woke us up a few seconds after I managed to get to sleep. He was always keen to be fishing at first light, so our dressing and advent upon the water were executed in pitch blackness.

The Saugeen River moved with ferocious determination. The steps we took were halting, made even more so by the fact that our legs soon froze inside the rubber of our waders. We clutched fishing rods in one hand and wading staffs in the other; such was the force of the river that it was hard to drive the stick down to seek purchase, the current kicking the tip away from the rocks below. I remember that the last of the night was leaving just as we achieved our destination some twenty feet from the safety of the bank. Here there was a run, a gouging of the riverbed, and as light came I saw that fishers lined the length of it. They stood upon the far side. Some had staked a claim on the rocks that broke the water's skin and seemed to make it even angrier. Many held long, long rods, fourteen feet in length, and they would leisurely lob a length of line upriver. Weight—usually a series of split-shot—would carry the bait to the bottom, where it would bounce along and attract the attention of a steelhead trout. Others—like myself—held shorter sticks, which meant that our line was thicker. On one of the longer rods, often called a noodle rod, you could get away with six-, even four-pound test, the added length of the bent stick absorbing much of the fish's force.

I now own a noodle rod. In fact, I own a number of rods for fishing steelhead, despite the fact that I rarely do it. I have the long noodle stick, and I have a thicker longish rod that I use with a bait-casting reel, which is how they do it on the West Coast. I own a couple of fly rods that I reserve for the purpose of steelhead fishing, although there is nothing remarkable about them. In my bag, however, are several fly reels devoted to the sport, metal wheels filled with shooting tapers, sinking heads, line that has been permeated with bits of tungsten to make it sink like stink.

(This might be as good a time as any to mention this deleterious aspect to the sport—the discipline—of angling. *The acquisition of fishing equipment becomes an addiction, even an illness.* We might be looking at behaviour best modified by a twelve-step program. I'll tell you a frightening story. Just last year, I went to the annual Sportsmen's Show here in Toronto. I wandered about gathering up fishing equipment. When I left the building, many people said to me things like, "Thinking of opening up your own tackle shop?"

(I nodded gleefully, seeking refuge in a kind of idiotic innocence, knowing that at home I already had so much stuff that I'd had to add an addition to the house to accommodate it. Not quite the truth, perhaps, but not far from it.

(I encountered an old friend, not seen for years, who said, "Looks like you're taking up fishing in a big way."

("Not really," I answered. "I've been fishing for a while."

("What's all this stuff for?" he asked.

("Various applications."

(These are the pitiful words of a tackle junkie: *various applications*. Let's see: on that day, I purchased a four-weight fly rod. That would be for small streams, you see. I bought a short, light action rod with a snazzy bait-casting reel. This would be for high-summer bass fishing. I bought a thick and pugnacious rod to toss huge, ungainly muskie lures. My muskie fishing is even more infrequent than my steelhead fishing, but I was in denial about that. I bought the West Coast steelhead gear mentioned above. I also bought my older daughter a little pink rod, and if I could have found one short enough, I likely would have bought one for the baby.

(I won't go into the terminal tackle. You often hear it said, by bucolic wags, that many lures are designed to catch fishermen, not fish. This is not the case with me. But if you hand me any bit of tackle, no matter how gaudily coloured and spangled, no matter how strange its construction, I will stare at it for a long time and determine an application. *This*, I might decide, will catch a suspended walleye. *This* will catch a blind bass. *This* will catch a carp that's depressed over a tragic love affair.

(Have I ever caught a carp? No. Do I have a vast array of carp-catching equipment? You bet.)

The cautionary aside over, let us return to the Saugeen River.

The anglers breasted along the runs were quiet and industrious folk, both young and old. The older ones—like my Old Guy—wore a lot of puffy outerwear, toques and mittens. The younger types were more fashionable, sleek in their Neoprene and Thinsulate. When someone took a fish, he wrestled silently for a moment or two, biting the tip of his tongue. The long noodle stick bent and quivered like a dowsing rod. Then the angler would step forward from the ranks as though he'd been selected for the next dance. "Fish on!" he'd low, and the others would silently reel in, or at least move their lines so that the grappler would have a clear path for the walk he was about to take. The fish would take flight downriver, and the angler would follow. Many times the fisherman vanished from sight; it was often a half an hour or more before he returned. The fish would, sometimes, be hanging from his body, dangling from his hand. Other times the fisherman merely assumed his spot in the line and recommenced flipping a tiny lure into the river.

The distant shore, far beyond the deeper runs, looked more appealing to me, mostly because it was much less populated. One of the reasons for this may well have been that it wasn't as good to fish, but that kind of thinking has never stopped me. It's an equation every angler has to work out for himself, a spot's productivity versus its human density. Myself, I favour emptiness, even if it means that the fish are few and far between. So I struck out for the far side, my gait as ginger and trepidatious as a Wallenda's.

By the time I'd achieved the middle of the river I'd had several near-death experiences. Much of my mind was concentrated on the wader-belt conundrum. My waders were cinched with a belt, which, according to some, would help keep water out of them should I succumb to the river's force and fall. Gordon, however, eschewed this belt, on the grounds that it would prevent him from freeing himself from his waders should he succumb to the river's force and fall. The obvious and best solution lay in not falling at all, but as the river got deeper, and stronger, it began to seem an unrealistic option.

That was when I noticed that salmon were rising all around me, their black humpy backs glistening in the water's boil. And I was distracted by this, as wonderstruck as a baby, so I waded through the fish with a serenity and sure-footedness that I never had had previously and have lost since, and I'll leave that stand as a little paradigm, an explanation as to why I like to fish.

Having achieved the far side, I began the process of lobbing my bait into the water over and over again, allowing it to bump along the bottom and into the maw of a steelhead. If you want to get a snack or a drink or anything, now would be a good time to do so, because not much happens for an hour or so. Izaak Walton points out that while hunting was denied to the clergy, angling was granted, and the reason, I'm sure, is that the repeated (and fruitless) action invokes a profound quiescence. And when this state becomes transcendental, just as the clouds are about to part and reveal the face of God, well, that's when the fish hits.

I should mention one thing about those black salmon, those single-minded dying fish with only eggs and milt on their minds. They have no interest in eating, so they allow the bait to bounce past them. Occasionally, however, the flash of pink or red will pull a little aggression trigger. The fish will lash out violently, and if you're standing on the bank throwing in your lure and basking in a hallowed calmness, the effect can be very dramatic.

I was fortunate enough not to allow the rod to be pulled right out of my hands. But I was jerked forward three or four feet; I stumbled forward and fell onto my knees, allowing a gallon or two of water to enter my waders. A point for the pro-belt faction, I suppose; if I'd had any more water in my boots I'd never have been able to accomplish what I did, namely, raising myself back onto my feet. The fish, meanwhile, was rocketing downriver, already some hundred yards away and across on the other side. I was reminded of my fishing etiquette. "Fish on!" I bellowed weakly. What had reminded me of the etiquette was the sight of fishermen leaping back in alarm as my fish plucked their lines like banjo strings.

It was time to begin the walk. Gordon never goes for these little strolls; to him it is a point of honour to stand your ground, to fight the fish with the rod and the line and gentlemanly physics. Myself, I decided to follow the fish, despite weighing, with the water in my boots, about four hundred pounds. I had also not adjusted the drag on my reel, a classic dunderheaded gaffe and one that I've repeated in many circumstances.

The salmon and I were separated by a couple of hundred yards at this point, an enormous distance, especially on a crowded river. I waddled strenuously over the rocks, sweat beading and then flowing into my eyes. The fish alarmed anglers with frenzied acrobatic leaps in their vicinity; it wasn't immediately apparent that this activity was related to the bloated fellow miles away who was fooling clumsily with his drag settings. Occasionally I would stop beside an angler, nod in the direction of my rival. "What do you figure?"

"I'd tighten up that drag some more and keep after him."

"Right."

We walked, my fish and I, a huge and complete circle in the river, and over time I managed to reduce the length of line that separated us. It seemed like many hours later—it was certainly close to a full one—that he lay panting at my feet, his caudal fin stirring just enough to keep him upright in a foot of water. I say *him* because when I tailed him and yanked him into the air, milt spilled from his belly. For a moment I felt achingly sad. That passed, and I merely felt deeply depressed by this act of onanism. The banks of the Saugeen River were littered with the carcasses of dead salmon. Females lay with their bellies ripped open, the roe pulled out and stuffed into little mesh bags. I sat down wearily with my dying fish at my feet.

I was startled to realize that people were applauding. Little crowds had gathered to watch my battle with the salmon, made all the more dramatic by my own ineptitude. I grunted by way of acknowledgement but could look at none of them. I picked up the fish again—it weighed seventeen pounds, but such considerations were somehow meaningless then—and killed it.

I complained, later, about the death on the side of the Saugeen River. I complained bitterly, as I had now added to it. I stood beside another angler and said, "Look at all the carnage down here."

"Yeah." He nodded at the dead black bodies, then he nodded at the fish ladder that ended the fishing grounds. "But it's no worse than the carnage up there."

I went up to look. In the waters of their conception, the salmon had completed their cycles and then expired, consumed and deformed by life. I was now undeniably part of that cycle, the perfect circle of life and death. Whether or not nature had intended me to be is a debatable point.

I wandered over to the fish ladder, a concrete construction that evened out the big rise, giving the fish a series of long, flat risers so that they could more easily achieve the higher ground. For half a mile below the ladder, the Saugeen River was thick with fishermen. The high morning had brought more anglers out, people with crude gear. Although it is illegal, many were snagging fish by dragging lures with large treble hooks across the riverbed, hoping to hook into the sides of steelhead or fresher salmon. Very few fishermen were catching anything. A creel count (not that anyone actually had a creel or would have been able to stuff one of these fish into it) would have indicated that the river was relatively empty.

Despite which, the fish turned up at the fish ladder in gleeful numbers. The river must have been teeming with life. Perhaps as anglers flipped their lures, steelhead and salmon were dodging the human legs like pylons. Perhaps they concentrated themselves in the middle of the river, running the gauntlet with grim single-mindedness. However they got there, they got there, splashing and bumping up towards their own particular heaven.

The ancient Johnson's watery demise was not immediately apparent because (a) we had no need of the outboard on that second day and (b) I wasn't quick to tell people about it. *They'll find out soon enough,* I reasoned, clinging in imbecilic desperation to the notion that total immersion in Murphy-whipped waters wasn't really bad for engines. *Hell*, I reasoned, *they make the things to stick in water, don't they?* So I kept the news to myself and breathed a sigh of relief when a decision was made to hike across the island to the larger set of rapids. This decision was based mostly on the weather, of such profound nastiness that only idiots would go fishing. Only three of us, Gordon, Paulo and myself, fit that description. We judged the distance overland to be half a mile or so, which seemed much more manageable than the waters.

"But what," I asked Gary suspiciously, "are you going to do here by yourself?"

"Oh, you know," he answered vaguely, waving his arms about the campsite for added vagueness.

"You're going to work on your damn journal, aren't you?"

"I might write a few things down, I guess."

"You know what, guys? I think I might just stay back with Gary."

"Come on, Kew," said Gordon, "let's go." Paulo strode off, his long legs chewing up lichen-covered rocks (remember, that's all we had for ground). Gordon wasn't so quick to strike out. He first of all cocked his head in the air, like a hound dog trying to pick up a scent. He then twisted his neck, sharply and suddenly, in a number of different directions, as if being hailed by voices that he alone could hear. Then, smiling with evident satisfaction, he struck out for the rapids, and I followed behind.

A walk through the world is different with Gordon. He comes across things, surprising and delightful turns of Mother Nature's, but rarely is he surprised by them. He often gives the impression that he himself put these things there, years before, looking forward to the day when he might reclaim them. "Here it is!" he'd say. "Sphagnum." He'd bend down and pick up a piece of the moss, then he'd hold it in front of my eyes and gingerly pick it apart, so that I might better understand the care with which it was put together. He'd offer me a piece, silently, solemnly, and I'd repeat the process.

Mostly, though, the treasures he sought and found were various fungi. Gordon is an avid mycologist, a collector of mushrooms. He collects them in the shadowed heart of the forest, and he collects them from the manicured lawns that line residential roadways. He digs them out of the dirt with a knife that is always secreted about his person. He professes that he takes great care in his selection, and I have no real reason to disbelieve him, no concrete evidence that he has ever killed anyone. But Gordon feels compelled to point out all the heinously poisonous mushies as he carves out his own. He likes to speak of grisly death by foolish ingestion. Having done that, he generously offers forward a huge bag full. "Fry them up with a little butter and salt," he says, and you search his eyes for the telltale glint of homicidal madness.

On this day he found slippery jacks. "That's a four-forker!" he told me with delight. He instructed me as to their identification, turning quite scientific on me, which he can do with the unsettling glazed eyes and monotonic speech of an idiot savant. "It belongs to the *boletus* family."

"And it's not poisonous?"

"Not poisonous, no." Gordon did, however, dig something out of the lichen, hold it up to his eyes as if reading the label and then grunt cryptically, if indeed anyone can grunt that way. Gordon threw this new mystery 'shroom into the plastic bag (it is nothing for Gordon to come up with a plastic bag, especially when decked out in his fishing gear, although I'm fairly confident he could produce one from his pyjamas) and we continued on our way.

The big rapids were larger than we'd anticipated. We'd seen them from the air, true, and Gary and Gordon had canoed up into the tailwaters in hopes of espying a camping spot, but we were still surprised, striking out of the bush and elbowing through the alder, at how much water there was, and how fast it was moving. Paulo had preceded us to the spot and was solemnly firing out a lure, once again using the pendulum method. One of the reasons he preferred this, I think, was that, because the idea is to let about a rod's length of line dangle down, the lure is always convenient for grabbing, deweeding and examining. Paulo needed to examine his lure and the line connection quite often, for it was common to get hung up on the rocks on the bottom. Paulo, for all his size and accompanying bluster, was a careful and meticulous angler. Not so yours truly, who has lost many a fish because of a nicked line. And Gordon, of course, is convinced that he's lost the world's record because he didn't change a frayed leader. So if there's any reader out there who was hopeful of actually learning something about fishing from this book, there it is. *Run your fingers over the last couple feet of line and make sure there are no nicks.* Mind you, this knowledge is available elsewhere; indeed, I have read it in every how-to manual and angling magazine that I own.

Gordon moved upstream to get at the fresher water. It would have been more like him to cede that water to us, to enhance our chances, but after the day before, Gordon seemed more intent on catching fish. He pushed through the furze and periodically looked out upon the river, which seemed to have the breadth of the Mississippi. The surface boiled and puckered; there were swells and concentric circles. This was serious stuff. It had eaten away at the banks, so that in most places your first footstep placed you in three or four feet of raging water. There was, however, a rock rising out of the water. It stood about thirty feet from the bank, large and flat and angled, a rock much like the one outside Copenhagen whereon languishes that fey girl. That's where Gordon fished from that day. Most of his angling time was spent getting to it.

I fished about a hundred yards downstream, using the fly gear. I stood in water up to my chest and roll-cast a length of line upstream. The Despair would skitter along the surface like a frantic water-walker. If a brook trout wanted it, he'd have to hustle butt. So I tried throwing a series of S-curves into the line, in hopes of delaying the bellying of the line long enough to get the fly down. I did in fact get semisuccessful at this, although there were no takers.

Gordon, I was curious to see, did much of his fishing from the same position as the Copenhagen girl, half-stretched out on the rock, one leg curled up beneath him, the other pushed out straight. I had not seen him fall, although this is what had happened. Halfway along on his journey to the rock his wading staff had become wedged between two rocks and the water had bowled him over. He'd smashed his knee on a rock and was favouring it now by laying the whole limb out before him. It was an awkward position from which to cast, but Gordon was managing it. He was throwing plenty of curves, too, mending the line, so that his Despair dove down towards the rocks. But he took no fish.

It was at this point that we began to have fishermen's dreams, which all involved being elsewhere. Mine was likely the most modest; I merely wanted to be on Gordon's rock, which was reasonably dry (the world was wet with rain, of course, but not as wet as the river) and afforded a casting platform, plenty of room for the back cast. Paulo had noticed that a little creek flowed out of the land across the river and decided that fish would congregate in the confluence in great numbers. There was no way of getting across to it that day, and such was the force of the river that it would be hard going under any circumstances. And Gordon—fishless, that day, with only the brilliant purpling of his knee for a reward—wondered where the brookies were. He began to think about the Old Place. Dangerous stuff, of course, and he was able to put it out of his mind.

"Tomorrow," he told us, "we'll get in the canoe and motor up to the next set of rapids."

"Good, Gordon!" said Paulo with great enthusiasm.

"Good," echoed I, with less.

On the return trip, Gordon's knee forced him to wield his wading staff with every footfall, like a Biblical patriarch. He began huffing and puffing with his second step. Paulo knew no way of tramping through bush other than at top speed, so those two became separated almost immediately. I tried my best to be some sort of connection, keeping stride with Paulo and then turning around, running towards Gordon briefly, waving my arms and blowing on my whistle. (Those whistles, remember, were a late-minute addition to Gordon's list and a damned clever one, except for the fact that Gordon himself seemed incapable of hearing them. I had the impression that you could toot one right next to his ear without drawing a response.) It wasn't long before Gordon was lost. Paulo stepped up onto a small rise and scanned the horizon, which was tree-filled and five feet away. "Oh, my goodness, where is Gordon?"

"If you're worried about where Gordon is," I demanded, climbing out of the bog I'd fallen into, "why were you walking so damn fast?"

Paulo made no answer, but I understood suddenly that he was having his own bristling difficulties with the Old Guy. His rebellion was subtle, and ran along the lines of the revenge sometimes enacted by children upon their parents, where a kind of fawning indulgence serves to clearly mark who is strong and who is weak, who is young and who is old. "Oh, my gosh, where is Gordon?" Paulo asked of me.

"Back there somewhere." I waved at the darkening furze.

"Oh, my gosh, will he be all right?" Paulo placed a cupped hand to the side of his mouth and bellowed. There was only silence in return. I executed a few plaintive whistle toots. Nothing.

"Does he have a flashlight, I wonder?" wondered Paulo, noting the fading of the light.

"I'll bet." Gordon walked around his house with the equivalent of a hardware store dangling about his person; I saw no reason why he would be less well equipped out in the wilderness.

"Gordon!" Paulo bellowed again, his eyes wide with alarm. "Come on," he said to me, "we must hurry back to camp."

We did hurry back to camp, although I'd be hard pressed to tell you why exactly. It's not as though there was a telephone there or anything. Perhaps we shared a notion that Gary would know better what to do, being as he was the most experienced outdoorsman. When we arrived, Gary was sitting on one of the green plastic lawn chairs, bundled up in most of his clothing, with an acoustic guitar balanced on his huge down-filled lap. He was staring at the fingers of his left hand, which were blue and trembling. "Useless," he muttered.

"We've lost Gordon," exclaimed Paulo. Gary—being a more experienced outdoorsman—cupped his hand around the side of his mouth and bellowed, "Gordon!"

"What?" came a voice, and Gordon stepped out from the furze behind the camp. He gestured with a bulging plastic bag. "Found more slippery jacks," he said. "It's a four-forker!"

"They thought you were lost," Gary mentioned.

"Lost?" Gordon snorted. "Oh, I got a bit turned around up there while I was collecting mushrooms, but then I just listened for the creek and found my way here."

The *creek* he referred to lay about a hundred and fifty feet to the east of the camp, a small foot-wide split in the island where the water flowed with all the power of postnasal drip. He could hear this quasi-rivulet at a distance of a quarter mile, but not a plastic toy whistle a few yards away.

I'll admit I had been fairly fearful, which is to say *confident*, that something bad had happened to Gordon. It had to do with my state of mind upon that island, which we might term low-grade panic. I was perpetually terrified that evil would befall us. My imagination could create quite gruesome misadventures. Prior to our departure, for example, I fantasized quite a bit about bear attack, going so far as to telephone Gordon and demand, without pleasantry or preamble, "Ever seen a bear up there?"

"I've only ever seen one bear in all the years I've been going up to the Broadback," he averred.

"That's good."

"Mind you," he continued, "it was the biggest damn bear I've ever seen."

"Oh?"

"Left behind the biggest scat. Enormous. And it was full of blueberries. Whole blueberries, hadn't hardly been digested. I was tempted to put them right in the pancake batter. I said to the fellows, I said, 'Hey, fellows, I'm going to put these blueberries—'"

"I've got to go now."

I was no longer afraid of bears; I had a hunch they hadn't survived the nuclear devastation that left us the only four men alive on the face of the earth. (This, notwithstanding a couple more reports by Gary of seeing something "large and white" moving about in the furze beyond the campsite.) But having put my mind somewhat at ease on the subject of far-fetched ruination, I began to speculate on the more commonplace: a twisted ankle, a shattered kneecap. I asked Gordon what we'd do if one of us—*me*— broke a leg.

"Broke a leg? Geez ... Well, I'd guess we'd put you in the tent, give you all the Percodan and the rest of us would go fishing."

This had, vaguely, the resonance of a joke, but he was entirely serious. I know that because, on one of his previous trips, Gordon had carried with him quite a serious bug from a casting competition in Spain. He fished one day, then collapsed the next. His fever skyrocketed; he became delirious, threw up constantly and was completely dehydrated from diarrhea. The other guys put him in his cot, made him comfortable and went fishing.

There was simply nothing else you could do, although I

kept trying to think of things. I had a small mirror with which I could signal passing aircraft, except that there were none. My ears became very attuned to the slightest sound that could indicate passing aircraft, and even though I heard none for the ten days I spent upon Murphy's Island, they remain so. It is amazing the small aircraft traffic here in Toronto, and I react to every passing.

There was another potential plan, taking the canoe and trying to get to Richard Demers's camp. This would take, we calculated, a day and a half. It involved going through or over many elevation lines signifying rapids or waterfalls. If we lit out for Demers's camp, it would be the act of desperate men. Only an emergency of the highest order would set us on that course.

Mind you, that was exactly what Gordon intended to do when he caught the world-record trout. A fifteen-pound brookie wouldn't remain that weight for long, either in captivity or dead, so it was Gordon's announced intention of jumping in the canoe and striking out for Demers's place so that the fish could be weighed at its heaviest.

I wasn't actively worried about this taking place. It's not that I no longer believed we were going to take the fish. I kept the faith burning. But when you've only seen two fish, a two-pounder and an eight-incher, it's hard to make plans against the eventuality of catching the largest one the world has ever seen.

I had more pressing worriments. Back at the camp, Gordon was sitting in his canvas chair, the plastic bag of fungi on his lap, a book held open in his mittened hands.

"Kew," he asked, "do you read French?"

"A bit."

"Tell me what this says." He thrust the book at me. The title I could interpret as meaning something like "Mushrooms of Remote Northern Quebec."

Gordon held the book open to where there was a picture of the mystery mushroom. "What does it say there?"

I scanned the dense paragraph for words like "*mort*" and "*angoisse*." I was reasonably certain the word for "convulsion" was the same (it is) but could find it nowhere. I pointed something out to Gordon. "I bet that '*diarrhée*' means 'diarrhea.'"

"I imagine so. But I think it says you won't get diarrhea."

I found the syntax a little confusing, so I couldn't speak with authority, but I did challenge Gordon on a point of logic. "Why would they specifically mention that you won't get diarrhea?"

"Plenty of mushrooms give people diarrhea. This isn't one of them. At least, I think that's what it says."

Gordon then made me help him clean the slippery jacks and their *quebeçois* kin, which I did with a feeling of, as I say, low-grade panic.

I should have recognized, I think, that the feeling was nothing unique to the island. I'd brought it with me from the big city, this pilot light for an all-pervasive dread. The only difference was that here on the island the little flame got fanned by Murph.

On that second night, Paulo and I took the canoe and paddled out from the wind-ravaged camp. We tilted the Johnson out of the drink, because we didn't have far to go, so that the craft bucked and bounced and bobbed. This was after Paulo had attended to his duties, which consisted mostly of alterations to the complex structure he'd already assembled, lashing together several of the branches, bolstering and shoring in an elaborate manner. Paulo had further girded the camp against the scorn of Murphy, and then he'd adorned the site with his rain-soaked laundry. Enormous woollen socks were festooned everywhere. Gary sat inside the tent and wrote in his journal, and I, not to be undone, rooted around in my baggage until I found the red virgin notebook I'd brought with me. I uncapped one of the virgin black pens. I sat down on my cot, across from Gary, blew on my hands a few times to dry and thaw them, and then I wrote, in my best hand: *Nothing has happened.*

It was kind of incredible, the extent to which nothing had happened. The barometer hadn't budged, despite claims to the contrary by Paulo, who periodically would take the instrument down with his huge hands and rap plaintively against the glass with his knuckles. The needle would vibrate slightly, like a feather stirred by the breath of a dying kitten. "Oh look!" Paulo would exclaim. "I'm not kidding you, it's going up!"

At any rate, I made this note, embellished the capital *N* until it shamed many an illuminated manuscript, and then Paulo and I went down to the shore, climbed into the canoe and went off in search of the pickerel we had been assigned to catch.

I think that we can learn something of the nature of angling by taking a brief little detour at this point in the story.

Some years ago, my friends from Wolverine Lodge and I stumbled across an article in *Field & Stream*. Strange and wonderful things were happening in a place called Greers Ferry, Arkansas. Specifically, huge walleye were being taken by the locals, and one weighing in excess of twenty-five pounds had bellied up and bobbed into fame, because this fish—you guessed it—weighed more than any other walleye ever seen by human eyes.

Greers Ferry, Arkansas, was quick to dub itself the "Walleye Capital of the World." The Chamber of Commerce announced a Walleye Festival and encouraged anglers from all over the world to come try their luck. They made it very tempting; should the world-record walleye be taken, the fisherman would receive fifty thousand dollars. If the fish broke the existing state record, the prize was merely a new boat, some twenty-odd feet of Ranger glitter propelled by a monstrous outboard, the kind of boat favoured by portly men who grasp little fish by the bottom lip, hoist them into the air and proclaim, "Now there's a *big* ol' bass."

We didn't really need such temptation, being Ontario pickerel boys from away back. In case there's any confusion on this point: walleye and pickerel are the same fish. The Americans use the former nomenclature—which has an undeniable descriptive rightness, given the opaque mystic quality of the eyes—whilst we frosty Northerners employ the antiquated "pickerel." This name is even a taxonomic boner, referring as it does to a diminutive pike. I can't imagine what cider-addled homesteader made this mistake; the fish clearly come from two different species. The pickerel is actually the largest member of the perch family, so why no one thought to call it, say, the percheron, is beyond me.

Pickerel are the most popular sport fish in Ontario, chiefly because they taste good, although some think them not much fun to angle for. They tend to be a bit fatalistic after being hooked. They come almost willingly boatside, and whatever thrashing they do seems more petulant than anything else. Skill is required, however. They are finicky creatures and will spend a long time pecking and lipping the bait. At such times it is quite easy, and common, to pull the hook right out of their mouths, causing the angler to feel foolish and the fish to think, "Aha! I *knew* something was up."

So for many years we have pitted our patience against their persnickety ways. We being the boys from the Wolverine Lodge, who, for the purposes of these pages, I will identify as Jumper, C.P., Dolpho and the Professor.

I can't remember who first saw the article in *Field & Stream* about Greers Ferry, Arkansas, and the fat dead fish, but the magazine was passed from hand to hand. At Christmas parties we would dream about taking those brutish pickerels, those aquatic percherons. We weren't even terribly concerned with setting a world mark and claiming the fifty thousand; we all agreed, however, that the boat would look very nice decorating the lodge's dock.

So on a bitterly cold day in February, we flew out of Toronto, Ontario, and landed—after a stopover for oysters and beer in Chicago—in Little Rock, Arkansas. We immediately peeled off outerwear, offering up winter-blanched arms and legs to the sun. We rented a car and drove a couple of hours to the north.

We stopped at a tackle shop just the other side of the bridge that Billy Joe McAllister jumped off of. The proprietor, whose name I remember as Woody, stood behind a counter of improbable messiness and smiled inscrutably whenever we asked him questions. He didn't seem unfriendly; he seemed at the same time amused and saddened by our queries, but unwilling to respond, for the wisdom of the ages has a tendency to shatter men's dreams. He did mention the cold front that was moving in, holding up a long pale finger and gesticulating vaguely at the Arkansan sky. I, for one, was not surprised. The Cold Front is by way of being a fishing buddy of mine, and I don't think I've ever embarked on an expedition without its company.

Woody mentioned, "The boy fishes," at about the same time we noticed a small pale creature moving amongst the dusty sporting equipment.

"Oh, yeah?"

The creature nodded.

"What," someone ventured in an affable manner, "do you fish for?"

"Wyatt Bias," answered the boy.

Greers Ferry, Arkansas, was a golf course. If there was a town there, I never saw it. I saw only the golf course, our lodgings (a multi-bedroomed condo that faced the greens) and the nearby marina. At the marina, several long-faced anglers stood around and complained about the lack of fish. The marina owners were quick to defend the fishability of Greers Ferry. "There's plenty of fish here," they said. "They're just a little hard to find."

Indeed. The fishery was created when the Corps of Engineers flooded out a river system, creating three bloated fingers of water, thousands of square miles of water.

Polaroids adorned the walls, pictures of men, boys and the occasional woman holding up big piggy pickerel, their huge marbly eyes full of camera flash, because all of these photographs were taken at night. We sooned learned that this was the local lore and custom, night fishing, what we called the Black Art of the Angle, an arcane pursuit. The idea was to journey to the end of one of the three arms, into the heart of darkness, and to pull a crank-bait through the clustering walleye.

We rented a boat, climbed in and set off upriver. The Cold Front made it just in time to join us, jumping in the battered aluminum skiff and saying, "Hey! You guys remember to pack your long johns?"

As I say, there were thousands of square miles of water, so it took us some time to select the six square feet that we would fish intensively. For we had determined to fish as we always did, proud Ontario pickerel men. Our favoured strategy was to tip a lead-headed jig with a minnow—a prissy way of saying "poke a hook through a little fish's lip"—and set this near the bottom. The jig-head itself would glow with brilliant chartreuses, pinks and various mottled pastels, drawing the glassy-eyed prey. I recall that at the time I possessed a sheet of shiny stick-ons, which I would affix to the round bead of lead so that it seemed to possess eyes. So this is what we did, and we did it at a place that seemed most to resemble our home river. Our choice was not made without logic, although it may well have been faulty. We knew how pickerel were supposed to behave, although they never do. For example, any number of people will claim that pickerel are a schooling fish. The fish themselves seem never to have learned this. What little success we had generally had to do with one of us picking up a nomadic singleton.

As I say, the fishery at Greers Ferry was made by flooding out a river system, so water covered much that Mother Nature would have left dry; cliffsides, for example, and cave-riddled scarps. The caves gripped my jet-lagged imagination. (We hadn't gone through any time zones, but I'd managed to over-imbibe on the flight, giving myself a hang-over with a five-day half life, so I'm counting that as jet lag.) The pickerel, I reasoned, were lurking in those caves. I devised various ways of angling for them, none of which I could actually put into practice. My point is, we caught no walleye pickerel, not that day, nor the subsequent day, nor the third.

And meanwhile the Cold Front was hanging around like a salesman in a snowstorm. I remember one night—we'd begun to indulge in the Black Art of the Angle out of desperation—as we sat in our tin tub, I was so cold that it truly made me feel a little warmer to *look* at the fires of the locals, some hundred and fifty feet distant. The locals persisted in their ways, standing on the shore and firing out crank-baits, wooden and plastic replicas of tiny fishes, but they didn't appear to be any more successful than the Ontario crew.

Despite which, every day more Polaroids would show up on the marina wall, angler and walleye caught in flash and moonlight. The beasts were truly magnificent, large and golden and muscular; the images gave us whatever intestinal fortitude we needed to climb back into the tub and make the long journey to the river's end, where we would freeze our butts off and catch no fish.

We met, one day, a sloe-eyed Minnesotan, who pulled his glistering boat up to the dock, jumped out and looked forlorn.

"No fish, eh?" we commiserated. He nodded. "So," we demanded conversationally, "what brings you here, anyway?"

"Read the same damn magazine you guys did."

That's essentially the story I wanted to tell, because we

are closing in on a truth about fishing. But before I get to it, I will tell you an ending, a relatively happy one. (This is not the official ending to the Arkansas story, which involved three-fingered shots of bourbon and a drunken car ride to fetch pizza. That's not as bad as it sounds; there were actually no people living in any of the other condominiums. It was just us and, across the way, a pizza place. It was kind of laboratory conditions for studying drunk driving. So I went to fetch the pizza, mostly without mishap, although I did manage to back into a tree as I pulled out of our driveway. In the morning, we looked and could find no tree. "Unless it's that one away over there across the road," suggested Jumper. "Naw," said I.) Anyway, we were sitting in our boat in Arkansas, on a day when the sun had managed to break through the clouds. We were, for the first time in ages, relatively warm. We dangled baits of various sizes over the side of the boat. A couple of us, Jumper and I, were firing crank-baits at some deadwood that poked up closer to the edge. It was a startled Jumper who mentioned quietly, "Fish on."

"Fish? You mean those finny things that swim around in the water?"

Jumper worked his rod and in a short while we were examining his prize, a good-sized specimen that appeared to be some sort of albino largemouth.

"Hey, I know what it is!" I recalled Woody's boy and his strange quarry. "It's a Wyatt Bias!"

Just then Woody and his boy came down the river in a small boat, smiling cryptically and firing plugs at the stands of rotting wood. We joined in. And that is how we came to catch white bass in Arkansas, a pursuit not without its charms, but it remains a huge and hideous fact that we travelled far to take pickerel, and we caught not a one.

Paulo and I pushed out and rode the Murphy-whipped water. We had thought to travel to the island that blocked the mouth of the large rapids, but Murphy had other ideas, chiefly, that we remain about a hundred yards directly off the shore of our camp. Paulo and I each had a rock tethered in nylon cord, and we pitched them overboard. Even so the canoe was dragged around by Murphy. But in time the rocks got purchase and we were stopped.

I tied on one of about four lead-headed jigs that I'd brought along. It had, I think, a chartreuse head. Lacking live bait, I pushed a Mr. Twister onto the hook, a little piece of rubber that imparted a little bit of motion and allure to the presentation. I set this bait on the bottom, which seemed to be about twenty feet below me, raised it up a few inches—all this is common practice, even unthinking habit, to an Ontario pickerel hunter—and waited. Momentarily. I felt the visitation of a walleye. But this was a much more insistent and dynamic sensation than I was used to. This fish mouthed the bait thoroughly. I then expected the fish to disappear, seeing as I had no meat to offer, but this fish seemed to exclaim, "A Mr. Twister? I *love* that shit!" The fish took the bait into its mouth and lit out for the territories. I pulled up emphatically, setting the hook, and then I mentioned quietly, "Fish on."

"Fish?" screamed Paulo. "Yahooo!"

Yes, sir, and for a pickerel, this was a strapping, spirited fellow. There was no woeful fatalism here; this guy swam off in all directions, jerking his head with pugnacious fury.

I boated the fish, which weighed perhaps two pounds. It was chubby and hale, a beautiful burnished gold. (The French name for the pickerel is *doré*, reflecting this coloration.) Paulo and I immediately sunk jigs down to the bottom. These fish seemed to know the scientific thinking; they were *schooling* fish and, by god, they actually schooled. The pickerel came and pecked—some evidenced the species' trepidation, gently mouthing and then spitting out—and many were caught. Murphy was actually aiding in the process, messing up the surface of the water so that we couldn't be seen down below, making sure that we jigged our bait in a rhythmic manner. Paulo hooted and cheered like an amphetamine-crazed cowboy. And that is how we came to catch pickerel in the middle of northern Quebec. So I guess the angling lesson to be learned runs along the lines of, *You can't always get what you want, but it's a good idea to have a Mr. Twister handy.* No, that's not right. The lesson is, you *can* always get what you want—it may just be on another part of the planet.

"Time me," said Gordon, brandishing a black-handled filleting knife. Paulo was busy festooning woollen socks, Gary was writing in his journal and I was, well, I wasn't doing anything, but I didn't cock my wrist to time Gordon, not wanting to get too involved in the fish-cleaning procedure. Paulo and I had returned to the campsite with six chubsters, enough for at least a couple of meals. At least, that's what we told ourselves and the others, although we intended to devour all the fish that evening.

"Time me," Gordon repeated.

"Go."

Gordon cut through the fish's head until it was nearly off. He made some surgical incisions down the length of its back. He then put the knife aside and wrestled the fillets away with his bare hands. He took up the knife again and flayed the pieces, separating the thin golden skin with a precise and gentle back-and-forth motion. Finally, he removed the fine bones from the rib cage and tossed the slabs onto a plate.

"How long?" Gordon wanted to know.

"A minute and fourteen seconds."

"That slow?"

"Yeah." I hadn't really timed him, but I thought a minute-fourteen sounded like a reasonable time.

"It usually only takes me thirty, forty seconds."

"Well, your hands are cold."

"You try now." I guess the nature of Old Guy lore is that it's kind of inclusive; the recipient doesn't get to pick and choose. I picked up a fish and did as Gordon had demonstrated. Twenty minutes later I held up two bloodied tatters of walleye meat.

"It takes practice," noted Gordon. "I remember once, they had a big fish-cleaning competition at one of the very early Sportsmen's shows. It may even have been the first one. There was, let's see, Ken Clappe from Skinner Sports, Charlie Pierce, who else, oh um, Norm Telfer, who at the time was vice-president of the Anglers and Hunters or some such thing. There was King White from the *Star*. And they asked me. We had four perch to fillet and we were timed and judged on neatness. I'm afraid I won on both counts." Gordon flipped another pickerel onto the cooler lid that we using as a cleaning surface. "Try another one."

I began to carve up the fish's body, taking greater care.

This time the fillets were thicker, much more geometric. I slipped the knife between the flesh and the skin and then—as my Old Guy had instructed—I pulled the skin rather than pushing the knife. Seconds later I held a freshly flayed piece of pickerel skin. Even I was impressed.

"Good job, Kew," said Gordon. He wandered off to find the skillet. I reached eagerly for the next fish.

The weather remained unchanged the next morning, wet and rainy. Still, we rose with some enthusiasm, because our plan was to hop in the motorized War Canoe and journey to the fishing fields. I was the least enthusiastic, my spirit weighted by my secret knowledge of the engine's immolation. After breakfast we donned our fishing gear, climbed into the canoe. Gordon yanked on the cord. The old Johnson spit up a bit of stale water, shuddered in a mechanical manner that made me think it might possibly have survived the ordeal. Ten minutes later it was doing the same thing.

Gordon emitted a quizzical nose whistle. "Wonder what's the matter?"

"Well," I ventured, "I think it might be a little *wet.*"

The motor was hauled up onto dry land. Paulo tore down a tree and lashed it crossways between two others, and we bolted the engine upright so that it could be operated on. We tore off the cowling and stared into its innards. When we pulled on the starter rope the motor would produce small, consumptive coughing sounds. Occasionally it would shudder and bark, stringing together enough of these coughing sounds to fill one's heart with desperate hope. Then it would expire once more, dying like a young female character in a Charles Dickens novel, for no apparent reason but with conviction.

What I know about outboard motors is negligible. The only knowledge I have was gained in those days in remote northern Quebec, when I stood around with Gordon, Gary and Paulo and stared into the mysterious greased bowels of the thing. I know that when you pull the starter rope a little ratchet gizmo flies up on a spindle, digging its teeth into a larger cog. I know that owing to the number of times I yanked the starter rope. I was, however, responsible for getting the engine started. A memory—perhaps from some former life— manifested dimly in my consciousness. I recalled seeing someone, in a similar situation, pouring a bit of gasoline directly into the carburetor.

I suggested this, speaking in a dull monotone, channeling the words of Fredo, an otherworldly garage mechanic. Gordon and Paulo both lifted their eyebrows. "Yes, you could try this," said Paulo, almost as though there was something unseemly, underhanded, about the idea. A small bit of gasoline was poured into the carburetor. I yanked the starter rope and the old Johnson roared anew. We sent up a whooping war cry and prepared to go fishing once again.

Preparing to go fishing took several minutes, as we donned waders and fishing vests and affixed accessories to our chests. We crawled into the huge plastic bag that protected our stuff from the rain. Just so I don't have to mention this again, it was raining. There was a period of about twenty minutes on the second day when it stopped. The sun made a glorious appearance, but it was like a movie star in a shopping mall: the sun waved, signed a few autographs, fucked off. So our gear was kept dry in this huge (ten feet square, something like that) plastic bag. Murph liked to open up this bag, knocking away the Coleman oil cans we used to seal its lips. Murph liked to bare dry things for the slanting rain. It was his hobby. So when you crawled into the huge plastic bag to retrieve things, they were usually soaking wet, and required shaking off and/or wringing out.

When we were finally finished the act of preparation, enough time had elasped that our breasts were no longer swelled with hope as regards the old Johnson motor. At least, this was the case with Gary and myself. Gordon and Paulo were still giddy with excitement. They pulled the engine off its tree stand, raced down to the waterfront and plunked it on the War Canoe. They loaded the boat with fishing equipment. They jumped in and grinned at Gary and myself.

"Get in!" they shouted.

"Shouldn't you see if the engine works?"

"It works, it works," said Gordon, annoyed at this breach of faith. "I can tell just by looking at it."

"I think," said Gary, "that you should try it, just to make sure."

"Get in the canoe," snapped Gordon.

"Just, um," Gary spoke softly, "try it."

"Push us off, Paulo!" shouted Gordon, and Paulo did so, placing his paddle into the rocks and throwing the canoe some twenty feet away from the shore. Gordon then pulled the starting rope.

Gordon was still pulling the rope as Murphy pulled the canoe around the bend of the island. The engine's consumptive coughs had become even weaker, as though it had had a lung removed or something.

Paulo and Gordon returned about an hour later. They

came by shore, Paulo knee-deep in water and towing the canoe behind him, as paddling was useless in the face of Murphy's scorn.

We put the engine back up on the tree and continued our existence, which was informed mostly with motor-futzing.

We explored the island.

There was a sense in which we were shipwrecked, after all, land-stayed until the plane came to fetch us. Any angling we wished to do—other than the rodeo-style pickerel fishing—was confined to the two sets of rapids that bracketed the island. Neither had yielded much in the way of fish, mind you, but it's not as though we had a lot of options. Plus—and this was a very attractive notion—getting dressed up to go fishing and then hiking through the furze was the one sure-fire method of getting warm. Especially hiking with Paulo, who bestrode the world mightily, trampling down the brush, making the earth tremble with his mighty size thirteens. I would huff and puff many yards behind, stumbling over the island's gnarly undergrowth, my face lacerated by the backlash of Paulo's trampling. Occasionally Paulo would stop and take his bearings with a small pocket compass, allowing me a short opportunity to catch my breath. Paulo would stare at the face of the instrument; he would look up at the treetops, down to the compass once more. He'd tap the glass face of the navigational tool, making the silver needle bounce. Then he'd set off in whichever direction he'd been headed in the first place. After three or four days, Paulo and I had more or less complete knowledge of the island, because we'd wandered every square yard of it. The main topographical feature was a ridge that rose behind our campsite and made a semicircle around the rest of the island. One day, headed for the small rapids, we scaled this ridge and found an abandoned campsite.

The bones of the site revealed that the camp had been methodical and orderly, the main construction having an imposing and correct squareness about it, especially in comparison to the addled gazebo we had managed to lash together. There was no garbage strewn around. An odd pyramid stood nearby, at least its wooden skeleton. This campsite was protected from the elements. It was about fifty feet from the rapids, and *it was already there*. It was already there when Gary and Gordon paddled around looking for suitable camping spots and, once we'd discovered it, the path from the rapids made itself patently obvious.

We told this news to Gordon, who was fishing down in the rapids. I suppose this means it was a day when Murphy was no longer in a frenzy, and if I had notes I could refer to, I'm sure I could relate that Murphy did calm down after six days or something, that he downscaled himself into a bracing freshet who meant us no greater mischief than making sure we were never warm. I believe what happened on this particular day was that Paulo and I had traipsed overland, whilst Gordon and Gary paddled the War Canoe around the edge of the island. Those two were down below, flinging tin into the water, when we descended from on high with the news of the ghostly abandoned camp.

Gordon nodded serenely, as though so connected to the universe that he was incapable of surprise. (This was the same man who suffered massive coronaries whenever little fish darted out from mossy cuts.) I'll admit it wasn't the most earth-shaking news, even if astounding that other human beings had ever tolerated the hardships of Murphy's Island.

Paulo, though, was giddy with discovery. Gordon asked him a few questions about the site. Was there, he wondered, another structure nearby? Paulo shouted that yes, yes there was! He proceeded to describe it, using his hands to suggest its shape and stating (then revising) the dimensions. Gordon waved a hand, silencing the lad.

"That's for drying pelts," he said. "It must have been an old Indian camp." Some of the Cree, Gordon explained, are still nomadic. Small hunting parties tend to hunt a place until all the hunting is done; they then move on, allowing the land to fill up again.

One time at the Old Place, Gordon began—this sort of nostalgia was creeping into his conversation more and more frequently—they had been sitting around eating dinner one night. (In the telling, Gordon began to work out exactly who the men might have been. Was Gary there? Was it the year Gary's father had come? Had Gordon's great friend Jack been sitting near the fire quietly? Then he shook his head, as if memory were too great a burden.) Anyway, they'd heard gunfire, the reports echoing steadily throughout the world. And suddenly there were ducks, although they hadn't taken wing; they were skittering along the water in panic. Every few seconds the bunch of them would settle their fannies in grateful relief, but then another cannonade would have them screaming and flitting off towards the next brief respite. Behind this brace of gaga waterfowl came a huge canoe. There were two men, their hair long and black, both dressed in the leather of a motorcycle gang. One of them was very little, and he had the job of propelling and steering the canoe. The other man, very large, stood bolt upright in the bow, his rifle held steadily, and fired at the scudding birds.

It was hard to say which group was more surprised, although neither wanted to show it. Gordon's friends continued eating. The Indian man in the bow lowered his rifle briefly but then raised it again, aiming at the ducks, singulary unmindful of anything that might be in sight and range. Gordon, typically, waved them ashore.

The two parties next exchanged baffling questions in their own languages. I suppose it likely that there might have been some stumbling middle ground (French, I'm assuming), but neither thought of it. They persisted in their individual foreign tongues, so that the exchange had a kind of historical resonance. Finally the Indian men, boring of it, dropped the conversation and walked through the camp, inspecting the white men's gear and pronouncing judgement. If they liked something, which was rare, they would purse their lips and nod judiciously. Usually, though, they would bray with derisive scorn. This is what they did when they came to the sleeping bags hanging up to air, and to the Coleman stove. Gordon's friends merely watched all this, sometimes smiling along, even laughing at a statement mumbled in the strange tongue. Gordon, however, took note of an audible squishing sound. He pointed, then shouted to the big man, "I can fix those!"

The large Indian man tilted his head, looked down at his feet, at the old black rubber boots encasing them. He looked up again at the little white man, wondering what he was saying, because if it had anything to do with the fact that the boots had holes in them, that his feet were wet, cold and puckered, he wanted to know. The big man took one boot off, offered it forward.

The little white fellow disappeared into the tent and emerged with a little box that he kept shut with pieces of exploded tire. He opened it up and took out more pieces of rubber and tubes of goo.

A little while later the big Indian man stepped hesitantly into the water. His little companion opened his mouth in order to bray derisively, but the big man silenced him with stabbing eyes. The Indian men waved at the white men, climbed back into the canoe.

The birds, meanwhile, huddled in a trembling brace a hundred feet away. At the crack of the rifle they shrieked and skittered away across the world.

It was on the trek where we discovered the abandoned Indian camp that I cleverly lost the top part of my spinning rod. I was carrying the assembled stick facing behind me, and I suppose one of the uppermost guides got tangled in furze and pulled away, taking that section of the rod with it. Once I discovered that it was gone—surely long after the fact of its disappearance—Paulo and I made an effort to reclaim it, but our search was useless. For one thing, Paulo's navigation had been less than precise. I was more able to retrace our steps than he, using such landmarks as, "Oh, here's where I tripped and fell on my face." For another thing, I was looking for a long thin piece of brownish wood. The floor of that island was littered with sticks and twigs. I tried to concentrate on looking for the metallic flashing of the ferrule, but most of the twigs also bore a peculiar branding of silver. I don't know what that could have been, other than a practical joke on God's part.

The long and the short of it was, I'd lost half my spinning rod, and I'd only brought my spinning rod along on this exploratory tramping expedition. Still, when we reached the water, I threw on a Mepps and tossed it into the water with my half-rod.

We fished the small set of rapids and then decided to round the cape at the bottom of the island; we could fish the larger rapids and presumably end up back near our camp. It was at the cape, then, that my Mepps got hit, slapped around really. The line went *bu-bump*, back and forth, and then the Mepps seemed to be spit back at me.

"Hmm," said I. Paulo stood a few yards away. "There seems to be something here," I said.

"Yes, a fish, I think."

"Probably." I threw the Mepps back into the water. My half-rod did not allow for a lot of distance, so the lure landed well within my sight.

The lure fluttered briefly and then was devoured by a pike. The fish at first blew by, as if en route to somewhere else, but then in a thrice it threw its head backwards, presenting towards me a white undermaw, and took the lure. There was a brief struggle that lasted a nanosecond. The fish won. I don't know if the fish was ever aware that we were locked in combat. It took the Mepps off to a pawn shop and left me trembling by the side of the water.

"That was a big fish," I mentioned to Paulo.

"Yes? How big?"

"Ummm ..." I was leery of overstating its size, because I had determined to catch the beast, and I did not want this accomplishment to be undermined by boastfulness. I therefore gave a very conservative weight of twenty-five pounds. Twenty-five pounds, you understand, was still monstrous. Truly, I thought the pike was more likely *forty* pounds, which would make it freakishly outgrown.

I saw that the cape made an excellent habitat for the ravaging pike; it could lurk around the corner, in slower water, and dart out into the discharge of both sets of rapids to nail little fishes and animals. For this reason I felt reasonably certain that the fish would be there the next day.

It would be somewhat devious of me to maintain suspense here, because the fish wasn't there the following day and I didn't catch it. I returned with my fly rod and trepidatiously cast a large green thing. (Those of you who expected more expertise concerning flies are bound to be disappointed. I tend to use either large green things or small green things.) The fly settled into the water. I gritted my teeth and waited for an explosion of considerable violence. I wasn't entirely sure what I was going to do once the pike hit. I had no leader, so even getting the fish on was going to involve a little luck. I had perhaps a 30-per-cent chance that the line would some-how escape the razor-sharp teeth. But after a few casts it became clear that the pike was off making its rounds.

On one of the last pikeless casts I pulled the fly back along the bottom and, quite by accident, it settled onto the top of an oblong, flat rock. This was perhaps fifteen feet away, plainly visible in the clean water of the extreme north. For a moment I occupied myself with making my fly hop along the rock's surface, jerking the line so that the marabou shimmied like a hula dancer. Then I thought, *That's enough of that*, and yanked the fly away, just as a fair-sized speckled trout ambled over to swallow the thing down. The yank alarmed the brookie, of course, and it swam away.

Pike—*Esox lucius*—figure into this story in more ways than one. The species represents a basic difference between my Old Guy and myself. I admire a certain crazed spunk they possess; Gordon only grudgingly acknowledges their existence. Back in those early days, it became clear that Gordon would have liked me to adopt this same disdainful stance. However, I continued to fish for pike every now and again, beating the waters around the lodge with gaudy wooden gewgaws. I kept this activity a secret from my Old Guy.

More serious rifts appeared. After Cincinnatti, I didn't want to compete in any more casting tournaments. I wasn't very good at it, but that was only one of the reasons. I just thought it was kind of a dumb pursuit. There was nothing in me that yearned for global domination. The club meetings were becoming less enjoyable, too, due mostly to Gordon's manner. He seemed to derive pleasure out of making us move en masse from one area to another. There I would be, fly-casting cheerfully, finding a gentle rhythm and grace that I possessed at no other time. "Okay, Kew," Gordon would bark. "Go line up for the bait-casting competition."

"No."

"Go line up."

"Tell you what. Give me five demerits on all the targets. That's my score. Now let me do this some more."

"It's time for the competition!" Gordon has no real debating skills except for force of will. Sometimes I would go line up with the bait-casting stuff and endure a bit of public humiliation, telling myself that it was good for the soul. (It is, too.) Then I began putting on my coat and leaving.

Then I began not showing up at all.

Thereupon followed a couple of years during which I had little communication with Gordon.

For one thing, my life suddenly acquired an alarming amount of busyness. I had written more novels, and they had proved more successful than my earlier efforts; I was offered work in the film industry. I met the woman I was to marry. My fishing became infrequent, although I still went to Wolverine Lodge and angled for pickerel and bass. I went to my father's place and took small trout out of the stream. I met others who shared my enthusiasm, and together we made forays into the land. And while I never amazed anyone with my angling acumen or ability, occasionally I'd do something that might raise an eyebrow, hint in some small way at an education with an Old Guy. Someone's fishing rod would prove difficult to pull apart, for example. I'd reach for it, hold it behind my knees with both hands braced and bracketed, and slowly spread my legs. The rod would easily and obligingly pull apart. (If it didn't, I had a plan B—get someone to assist. But, like my Old Guy, I'd advise that we both place a hand each on the female and male sides of the joint, lest the rod be broken.)

I recall that once or twice Gordon called me and asked when I might be coming out to the club. I said that I'd try to get out the following Wednesday, but I never did. And once or twice I called up Gordon; I'd be travelling to some new place, and I'd ask what local lakes or streams were fishable. He'd answer pleasantly enough, always eager to demonstrate his knowledge of the land.

The nadir of Gordon's and my relationship came a week or so after our first daughter was born. Gordon began to call, saying that he had something important to discuss with me.

He became quite insistent and wouldn't accept any of my gutless dodging techniques.

"Well," I'd say, "as soon as I know my schedule..."

"What about tonight?"

"Tonight is not good. Tonight there's a lot of stuff going on."

"What about tomorrow?"

He finally pinned me down, and on a winter's afternoon he came to our house. He spread a lot of computer-generated paper over the table, claiming that he was interested in our daughter's future. And while it's true that he maintained over and over again that the odds were overwhelming that Carson would live to be eighty-five years old, a lot of the computer-generated numbers had to do with the possibility of her death. I am superstitious enough to find such talk unsettling, even angering. For the first time in my life I refused to buy any insurance from my Old Guy. As politely as I could, I asked him to leave.

Then there was silence between us. This brought with it a sense of relief, almost of newfound freedom.

Although I'd wake up sometimes, in the dead of night, and remark to myself that I was up early enough to greet the dawn at creekside. I could jump into my own car, hightail it over to Scarborough. My Old Guy would be sitting in his car, sipping from a thermos of sickly sweet coffee. I missed that, sometimes.

Do you recall me mentioning Leonidas Hubbard, the subject of the fine book *Great Heart*? He set off to cross Labrador, taking with him his friend, the quiet and recently widowed Wallace, and the young native guide George.

Things didn't go at all well. They were underequipped (they had no shotguns, for example, only rifles, which undermined their hunting efforts) and overburdened. Their progress was arduous and minimal, just enough to get them lost beyond hope.

Some of Hubbard's journal entries have a kind of eloquence, a poetic economy, that I admire. Here is what he wrote on September 4, 1903:

Hard to keep off depression. Wind continues and all hungry.

This was our situation, to a certain degree. Paulo and I were hungry, although Gordon and Gary seemed satisfied enough. Gary was refined and civilized; Gordon, who had yet to pay a satisfactory visit to our latrine, was afraid to consume any more food. Not to mention incapable of it. But Paulo and I were actually losing weight, a fact we noted on the rare occasions when we changed into clean clothes. Bathing was an art little practised upon that island. On day four or five—I wouldn't know precisely without referring to Gary's journal—I could take no more of my own fetid aura, so I peeled away layers of clothing and raced into the lake. Such was my intention, at least, although with my first watery footfalls that intention disappeared, along with my breath and private parts. So instead I balanced on a rock and flung droplets of water upwards with cupped hands, then ran back to the campsite, declared the process "bracing" and climbed into my sleeping bag. When I did get warm enough to put on my clothes, many hours later, I remarked that I had cinched my belt on a new, untried hole. We were very active on that island, and although Gordon's cooking was superb, he only made three meals a day. So Paulo and I, large lads to begin with, were shedding poundage. We thought about food quite a bit, although not as much as Leonidas Hubbard had. Some days his journal entry was nothing more than a listing of the day's meals:

Pancakes, bacon and melted sugar at three o'clock—bully! Dried apple sauce and hot bread, bacon, coffee and milk for supper at eight-thirty—bully!

It was, just as Hubbard had noted, hard to keep off depression. Gordon and Paulo continued to work on the drowned Johnson. Gordon had changed its spark plugs half a million times. Paulo stared into its innards, tapped on grease-covered bits of ancient machinery with the nose of his screwdriver and eventually was ready to make a diagnosis. "Yes," he said, "it is wet."

This was difficult to contest. The whole world, as far as we knew or could see, was as soggy as a sock in a puddle.

"As long as it is wet, it is not going to work," said Paulo. "There is nothing we can do but wait."

With that, the three of us went about our business. Gordon continued changing spark plugs. As he did so, he first hummed, then whistled, then sang a little song under his breath. "Oh, yes," he intoned, "I'm the great believer..."

Paulo hung socks all about the crooked wooden structure he had wrought. Gary continued work on "A History of Mankind" or "A Dissemination of Philosophical Thought" or whatever the hell he was working on. I climbed into my sleeping bag, placed the earphones over my ears and listened to Beethoven's Seventh Symphony.

Other of that great man's symphonies are perhaps more famous—the histrionic Fifth, the gushing Ninth—but I think the Seventh was Ludwig's masterpiece. It is life-affirming—especially when you picture Beethoven hunched over at the piano, pressing his dead ears against the soundboard—but without a trace of piety. The contemporary critic Weber said that Beethoven was surely drunk when he composed the Seventh, and perhaps we should nickname it such, and add it to the list: the Eroica, the Pastoral, the Choral, the Drunken.

Beethoven's Seventh Symphony rarely fails to rouse my spirits, but it did on that occasion. Cutting through the music were harsh ack-acks, the last pitiful sounds of the drowned engine. Gordon refused to let it die and could not accept that the only course of action was to wait. Perhaps he thought, Wait for what? A good point. The sun had yet to make anything but the briefest of appearances. So Gordon continued to make what adjustments he could. He did this with such energy and determination that Paulo eventually went back to help, and Gary set down his journal, and I laid aside the little tape recorder, and the four of us huddled over the motor like surgeons over a bus-accident victim.

We found a linkage that seemed suspect; we'd pull it back with our fingers and let it go, and it seemed not to snap back with the appropriate military obedience. Gordon grinned.

"Kew," he said, "go into the tent, find that white knapsack, find a little plastic box labelled 'odds 'n' ends.'"

This was a disquieting notion, that Gordon was willing to label some of his collection as "odds 'n' ends." He must have collected detritus of such a vague nature that even he himself couldn't identify its origin or assign it a possible utility.

I knew pretty well where the white knapsack was: it was supporting the front end of my cot, so I always bore an impression of its flaps and clasps on my face. I removed it from that place, opened it up and, what seemed like some hours later, found the plastic box in question. It contained, in a curiously organized fashion, thin filaments of wire and tiny rubber rings, each component assigned to its class and a corresponding compartment. It was, as only luck of the highest order could have provided, a kit for fixing imperfect linkages within the bowels of a soggy outboard motor. Gordon, his reading glasses balanced on the end of his nose, worked with his fingers and produced a variety of odd noises through his nose. Sometimes Paulo would move to assist; sometimes the younger man would take over the operation while Gordon stepped away, putting on his thick mittens to warm his hands, staring at the Johnson with grave concern.

The linkage, in dry test runs, seemed to work a flap (I know, pretty damn technical) a little better than it had previously. Paulo went to yank the cord, but Gordon stopped him and moved forward to change the spark plugs one more time. He blew on the terminals, making sure they were as dry as our world would allow, then screwed them back in. There was a bit of squabbling here, with Paulo accusing Gordon of forcing the spark plugs, an unimaginable mechanical sin, thereby ruining the threads. Gordon snapped that he'd been changing spark plugs since before Paulo was born, and he'd never stripped any threads. I believe he actually may have in this particular case, but that's not the point. I only write of the spat to illustrate that nerves were frayed.

We took turns yanking the cord, because there was some

hint of combustion, an echo from deep within the chambers. At one point the engine actually seemed to turn over, just once, a splat that seemed to say, "I would live had I but a little more strength." Gordon knew how to give it that: by changing the spark plugs. (He didn't have an unlimited supply, of course. He seemed to have six that he replaced and recombined, hoping for an answer to the ancient puzzle.) Then I grabbed the cord, did the two-phase yank—back to the catching point, pause, then away in a straight and fluid motion—and the engine regurgitated black smoke and roared into life.

We fell upon our knees and gave forth great hosannas.

The engine ran for about a minute, suspended on our makeshift rack; we could not let it go any longer than that, because we had not provided it with water to cool its ardour. We feared it might seize up—actually, the other fellows feared this; I was and remain kind of ignorant about motors —so Gordon pressed the stop button.

Gordon grabbed the engine off the rack and began to walk down the pathway—which existed only in the vaguest way— managing to stay upright through the power of concentration. Paulo pulled the engine out of his arms. "No, Gordon. I will do this for you."

Gordon was too excited even to argue.

And then, with the same kind of silence produced by children up at six o'clock on Christmas morn, we began to put on our fishing clothes.

We knew where we were going, across Q Lake to our north, through a snaky section of river, to the Falls. The Falls had become our Elysium. There the speckled trout would be leaping gleefully, cavorting in the spray like Polynesian maidens in a bad movie. And there would be the big guy, fifteen pounds of muscle and colour.

Gordon, beside himself with joy, made a number of mistakes as he dressed, putting his long johns on over his pants, that sort of thing. Whenever he discovered one of his errors, he'd cant his head backwards and laugh towards Heaven, both delighting in his own littleness and defiant about it.

Fishing gear was eventually donned; angling equipment was corralled and thrown into the belly of the boat. We climbed into the War Canoe. Gordon wrapped his fingers around the grip of the start cord. He stared at his blanched knuckles for a long moment. "Think I should change the spark plugs?"

We murmured no.

But perhaps he should have. Gordon yanked the cord and the engine made the smallest of spitting sounds, as though the entire theory of internal combustion was as inconsequential as a sunflower seed. When Gordon yanked again, the old Johnson refused to make even that sound.

Gordon threw himself out of the canoe and up the pathway, thrashing through the alder bushes. We found him sitting on a rock, tears streaming down his face. He wiped at his nose and eyes, and leaky stuff got caught on his mittens; he smacked his hands against each other and pulled them apart, and the stuff got long and stringy, so that Gordon looked like a man trying to knit a scarf out of human misery.

"This trip was supposed to be so good," he whispered, "and everything's gone so wrong."

Coincidentally, Gordon's favourite trout fly was the Despair. That may seem like a glib segue, but I wanted to illustrate the awkwardness of the situation. I was not used to seeing my Old Guy consumed by sorrow.

The fly was developed, in the forties, by a man named Jack Sutton.

Sutton was an expert fisherman, a wonderful caster, a fine crafter of equipment, and it was his presence behind the counter at the Simpsons' fishing department that made it the mecca of local anglers. It was his presence that drew the teen-aged Gordon, who would hang around and pester the older man with questions, an acolyte at the feet of a wise Old Guy.

Except that Sutton was usually rather busy, and if he took time with every teen-aged kid who wandered in off Queen Street he'd never get anything accomplished. So he'd answer the boy gruffly, perfunctorily.

One day the kid pointed at the special rod suspended on the wall.

"What's that?"

Sutton responded without looking up from his tying vise. "That is the lightest fly rod ever made."

"Oh, yeah?"

"Yes."

The kid eyed the thing for a long moment. "What does it weigh?"

"It weighs an ounce," responded Sutton, "and an eighth."

"An ounce and an *eighth*?"

"That is correct."

"Why an eighth?"

"Hmmmm?"

"Why an ounce and an eighth?" demanded the kid. "Why not just an ounce?"

"Because if it weighed only an ounce, the rod would not be usable."

"If you can make one that weighs an ounce and an eighth," theorized the kid, "I don't see why you can't make one that weighs just an ounce."

Sutton completed the pattern he was tying, removed it from the small dainty jaws of the vise. When he looked up the kid had disappeared.

Gordon went home and began construction. He took a piece of bamboo, split it up and then began to plane the cane until it achieved paper thinness. Before tying on the rod guides, he dropped them into acid, let the stuff eat away some of the metal, fished them out again. He used the lightest thread he could for wrapping, the least substantial of reel seats.

And he took the rod down to Simpsons, went to the fishing department and showed it to Jack Sutton. Sutton waved it in the air, noting the sensation of power even though it felt as if he had nothing in his hand. Sutton put the rod on the scale, adjusted the weights, checked the tally and then looked at the kid.

"So," he asked, "what did you say your name was?"

Sutton would get to know the name well. It was, after all, Gordon who bested Sutton's Canadian record for fly distance.

Gordon's Despairs (the fly is so-named because "despair" is what the fly means to a trout) are slightly different from Sutton's originals. Sutton had initially been trying to simulate a crane fly nymph at the same time as he fooled around with a caddis pattern. The two gradually merged into one creation, combining the caddis' laid-back wings with the crane fly fan. Sutton also tied on a tail, although young Gordon never saw why.

"I don't see why you put on a tail."

"Because it looks good."

"Yeah," Gordon would nod uncertainly. "But those insects you're trying to imitate don't have tails in the larval stage."

"Is that so?"

"And why do you put on a tag?"

"To represent an egg sac."

"But there shouldn't even be an egg sac."

"Hmm. Is that so?"

Gordon continues to tie neither tag nor tail. "So," I once said to him, "you don't technically use a Sutton's Despair."

"Sure I do," he responded. "I would never call it anything else."

That night, the clouds parted over Murphy's Island. At least for a time. God pulled back the curtains and showed us one of His biggest hits, a bona fide blockbuster, a little thing He likes to call the Northern Lights.

I have recently learned that what one sees sitting at the top of the world is mirrored precisely at the bottom. If from Canada you see a certain silver shimmmy, Australians—those fortunate enough to be abandoned in the wilderness, far from cities—see the same silver shimmy. I question how scientists determined this. Have they been hooked up by telephone or radio, trying to describe each moment with the meagre human language? "Oooh! They're kind of all stabbing up now!"

"Stabbing! That's right! And now they're like curtains."

"Exactly!"

But such information runs contrary to the nature of the aurora. The northern lights are a unique and miraculous spectacle. The display we saw was robust and vigorous, and it had the theme of ascension. Light played first across the horizon, slightly to our right as we gazed out upon Q Lake, and then climbed upward with each new splash. Sometimes the light hung as thick as drapery in a suburban bungalow; sometimes it was a pale ephemeron and seemed as much a product of human imagination as—my science is inexact— refracted sunlight playing in the magnetic fields.

I raced into the tent, grabbed my Sony Walkman and walked back towards the water with the fourth movement of the Seventh ringing in my ears. The music seemed full of angelic yodelling. This was the piece of music that Wagner had called "the very apotheosis of dance," which means that at some point Wagner must have been standing out upon the hills, buck naked, waving his pale buttocks in the moonlight. I fixed the earphones on Gary's ears. He was a musician and, I felt, most likely to understand. But Gary had begun grinning as soon as the northern lights made their appearance, and nothing could stretch his mouth wider than it already was. I tried Paulo next. As I settled the earphones on his head a strange kind of look drifted across his face, as though he were a kitten transfixed by a sunbeam. And then Paulo turned towards Gordon, poor miserable Gordon, and placed the earphones upon his head.

Gordon's head snapped upright, much like that of a deer startled by the sound of a breaking twig. He reached up and moved the earphones until they nestled comfortably in the flaps and folds of his ears, and then he waggled fingers at me, bidding me turn up the volume. I did so until the glorious roar inside the Old Guy's head would have been deafening. Gordon gave me a thumbs up and bellowed, "Good!" so loudly that the word was still echoing many minutes later. He turned his attention to the aurora.

We awoke the next morning to the combined sounds of Gordon's singing—"Oh, yes, I'm the great believer..."—and French cooking as executed at $-3°$ C. The cooking sounds were of two sorts: a crisp clattering as pots fell out of Gordon's frozen hands, and then a clatter/scream combination as heated frying pans flew out of his hands, which were still frozen except for where the flesh was freshly seared.

Gordon herded us out of the tent and gave us breakfast: crepes covered with syrup from the suburban Scarborough maple. We hunkered down over our plates and tried desperately to ingest the crepes before they froze.

Gordon set his plate down and folded his hands. "Is this a good idea?" he began.

The three of us exchanged uneasy glances. To a query pitched so ominously the answer could only be no.

"The problem with the motor is, it's too wet. Correct?"

"This is correct, Gordon. Everything is wet inside."

Gordon waved his hand irritably at Paulo, who had failed to recognize the rhetorical nature of his statement.

"Okay." Gordon cupped his mittened hands before him, both as an aid to visualization and as a representation of the elegant rightness of his thinking. "Here's my idea. We wrap the motor in aluminum foil. Okay?"

I'd seen Gordon wrap a lot of things in aluminum foil,

although never anything as substantial as an outboard motor. Still, we all gently inclined our heads towards him, allowing this notion to exist at least as a possibility.

"We make a tent of aluminum foil, you see, for the motor. And then underneath it, we put the Coleman lamp. Fifteen, twenty minutes later, she's dry as a bone. And we zip down to the Falls and catch specks. All agreed?"

There was a chorus of what sounded like philosophical insects as we all went *hmmmm* in curious harmony.

"Do we have enough aluminum foil?" Gary wondered.

"Oh, yeah."

"This might work, Gordon!" enthused Paulo. "Yes! Because the motor would dry out."

Gordon smiled shyly. "Eh?" He wagged his eyebrows. "Is it a good idea?"

"It *seems*," said I, "like a good idea."

They all accepted my contribution as unqualified praise. They didn't seem to realize it was constructed along the lines of "John Wayne Gacy *seemed* like a nice enough fellow."

We did, remarkably, have enough aluminum foil to cover the ancient Johnson outboard. We moulded the stuff to the motor's contours and left a skirt at the bottom, even an opening through which we could insert the lamp. We lit the Coleman, pumped it until it glowed eerily bright in the midday gloom and situated it under the motor.

There was afterward some talk to the effect that somebody had wondered aloud whether or not we should drain all the gasoline out of the Johnson. Apparently—bear in mind, I have no memory of this conversation—Gordon thought this unnecessary. All I remember is the four of us standing back to watch the baking outboard with great satisfaction. The silver construct gave forth sizzles and sighs, water molecules being devoured by the heat of our miraculous lamp. The four of us held our hands towards it both for warmth and to show our adulation.

We had just turned away (I believe to don our fishing gear, so that when the bone-dry Johnson was unwrapped we'd be ready to go) when it exploded. The sound was not very dramatic, merely a pop such as the class clown might make with a finger and a chubby cheek. Visually the display was more impressive, with fingers of flame first clawing their way through the foil's thin openings, then disappearing to leave behind an unnatural glow somehow emanating from deep within the silver char.

We responded in various ways. Gordon, of course, tore off the aluminum foil, burning his fingers and crying out in great pain. I searched my memory quickly for the appropriate response to fire, coming up with *Stop, drop and roll.* I was in the middle of the third roll when I recalled that this was designed for those instances when you yourself were on fire, so I came up with plan 2: *Drench the outboard in water.* I grabbed an empty orange juice container and was down to the lake and back in a tick. Just as I was about to drown the motor a second time, Gary took a piece of soggy burlap and suffocated the flames.

Gordon went down to the shore and sat on a big rock, staring out at the world, deeply hurt by its betrayal. Murphy continued to rage, which is when Gordon yelled back, "Blow, you cocksucker, blow!"

He then fell very, very silent.

The three of us stood some distance away from the disconsolate Old Guy and shook our heads with clinical propriety, as if we were mechanics and Gordon a car that would not run properly. Gary made a tsking sound. "I've known him for twenty-five years," he said, "and I've never seen him like this."

"We must do something!" acknowledged Paulo. "Gordon is very sad."

"This is the only thing I can think of," Gary said. "We have to get down to those Falls. We're going to have to paddle down. Now, I think it's about seven miles. Two of us could make it easily enough. We could see how hard a paddle it is, and if it looks okay, tomorrow maybe we could all go down. That's all I can think of."

"Good idea," I seconded.

"Now," Gary went on, "who's gonna go?"

"You're the strongest canoeist," I pointed out.

"And Gordon must go!" said Paulo.

While both Gary and I nodded, we had our doubts. "I don't think he'll do it," said Gary. "I think he's too discouraged."

"We must ask!"

"We might as well ask," I agreed.

Our little clutch of mechanics sidled over to the Old Guy. He gave no indication that he intended to do anything—rise from the rock or continue breathing—ever again.

Gary explained the plan, staring towards the water, avoiding Gordon's eyes. He concluded by saying, "So we thought it was maybe the best idea if you and I went."

Gordon said, "Okay," and got to his feet.

I made them bagged sandwiches, threw in a couple of ice-cold fruit juices. (Our fruit juices were still ice-cold, by the way, owing to the new cooler Gordon had purchased for the trip, a block made out of sleek silver, ordinarily used in the transportation of human organs.) Gary and Gordon climbed into the canoe and set forth in search of fertile fishing grounds.

Our own fishing grounds, the rapids that framed Murphy's Island, were barren and cursed. We had taken two trout out of them, one largish, one minuscule, and we had seen but a couple more. I had grappled briefly with a monstrous pike. Pretty pitiful for more than a week spent in the bush. Still, with the older men gone and the day stretched ahead of us, Paulo and I looked at each other—only briefly—and began to climb into our gear.

"Oh," lamented Paulo, "I wish we were at the Old Place." I found such whimsy off-putting, but I let Paulo indulge because it seemed, unaccountably, to cheer him up. "We would be catching many fine fish." A wide grin came to his face, struggling beneath his moustache like a lifter shouldering a lot of weight. "*Big* fish. I would have a fine fish for my wall. Gordon would perhaps have the world-record fish."

Paulo took his compass out of his pocket, opened it, tapped on the glass front, pocketed the instrument. This was mere ritual; at no point had he bothered to look at it. He struck into the bush.

"We should have gone to the Old Place," said Paulo.

"They wouldn't take us. Propair couldn't fly us there."

"Ah," nodded Paulo. "Maybe," he suggested, "Gordon didn't fight hard enough to get there."

I saw that Paulo was trying to make this all Gordon's fault. I had absolutely no objection to that, understand, I just thought Paulo was way off in his analysis. "I'll tell you the mistake Gordon made," I said. "He thought Demers was trying to bullshit him. But why would he? Demers knew I was working on a book; does he want me to say, 'Richard Demers, who runs a fishing camp, sent us someplace where there were no fish?' No. He was trying to help. And Gordon couldn't see that, or wouldn't believe that. That's what screwed us up here. Gordon has no faith in human beings."

We knew now pretty much where we were going, so Paulo stopped only occasionally to open the pocket compass and tap on the glass. I trotted along behind him, huffing and puffing, falling to the ground every fifty feet as though trying to avoid sniper fire. We crested the rise by the abandoned Cree camp, descended the path that they had thoughtfully left behind for us. The collapsible boat lay in its brushy mooring, because we hadn't had a day of sufficient windlessness to attempt to return the misbegotten craft to the camp. That particular day, however, was approaching fineness, so Paulo and I climbed into the fold-up dinghy and paddled across to the other side of the river. We did this in a fury, fearful of being sucked through the rapids, but we were both big beefy boys—although, as I have mentioned, we were both a little less beefy than when we started the journey.

But it is time, you know, for lessons to be learned. The plane is due to arrive the day after next, after all. And the first and simplest of these lessons is, I complain too much. I was tempted to write, "We all complain too much," but I'll speak only for myself. I complain too much. I've written about hunger; I've written about losing an inch or so of pale milk-fed belly fat. But I fared much better than our friend Leonidas Hubbard, who starved to death. Their little trio had been forced to abandon much of its foodstuffs because it weighed them down, but after that they caught no fish (!)

and shot no game. So Wallace and George struck out through the snow to seek assistance, and Hubbard, too weak to follow, remained behind and starved to death. And even in the midst of this death, which he himself described as "not so hard," Hubbard was able to make this journal entry, which has the simplicity and grace of great poetry: *"Fine evening. Fine river. Fine world."*

The river this day was indeed fine. It was also damn cold, a discovery I made upon stepping into it. Apparently sometime during our trek across the island I'd torn a hole in my waders. This came as no great surprise; if anything, the surprise was that this hadn't happened before, because most of the alders possessed truncated limbs close to the ground, sharp little amputations.

Paulo moved up towards the headwaters. His determination to catch a mountie had not diminished, though it was liberally laced with despondency. So he marched up to where the water entered the chute, the first ripplings breaking on the surface. A small mound of turf blocked that entrance, and the current had carved its sides until it had become an apartment complex for speckled trout, or so one would have thought. The little brookies could have nestled in the shade, kept a sharp lookout on the faster water. So Paulo fished there first, methodically and beautifully.

Myself, I was somewhat restricted in that I couldn't (at least, was reluctant to) wade into the water. I spied a rock some distance from the bank, a large flat rock, plenty of room for a boy to stand atop. Getting to it didn't seem to require me getting wet much past the knee, and my little tear was two or three inches above that. So I achieved the rock, climbed aboard. The river spread out in front of me, a collage of foam and stone, the broken reflection of cloud and jewels of sunshine.

I peeled line away from the reel, dumping it onto the rock. Hey, I realized, this is pretty good. It was good because one of the problems with fishing a big strong river is that normally you can't dump your line, because normally you are standing in the river. The trick instead is to gather the line up in your left hand (if you're a right-handed caster), looping it into even coils. *Gather two, drop one* is what my Old Guy had taught me, and then as you cast you allow the line freedom to fly eagerly through the guides. I had some problems with this. It was, indeed, one of the things I was working on that August evening in the park. I tended to throw the coils towards the first guide in desperation, so that it bunched up like traffic at an accident site.

But standing on the rock, I could dump the line onto the rock and concentrate on the cast, the Double Haul.

The Double Haul is an Old Guy thing. As I've explained, Charles Ritz was the man who worked it out in theory, explaining the physics, how two emphatic pulls on the line at the reel—one on the back cast, one as the wrist breaks on the forward cast—would propel the line with greater force. Marvin Hedge and Myron Gregory designed the principle of forward tapering. Previously fly lines were either level or had a double taper. In the late forties, Hedge and Gregory came up with the notion of placing a thin silk-filled sleeve over a regulation line, loading the weight near the front end.

Gordon met Myron Gregory at a casting championship. The first time he saw him, Gregory was casting Double-Handed Salmon, the seventeen-foot rod. This gear is very unforgiving, and the smallest lapse of timing, the tiniest twitch of the rod tip (so very far away) will send the thick line into riotous rebellion. It usually sneaks up behind the caster and carves up his backside, continuing the crack of the butt until it meets the neck. This is what had happened to Myron Gregory, with even grislier results than usual. His back was more or less flayed. His shirt was rent, blood flowed copiously. His gillie (casting has appropriated the name of the man who assists Scottish fly-fishermen) was the late, great Buddy Tarantino. "Stop, Myron!" he pleaded.

"No way," replied Gregory, a huge man. He stood in the box and completed his game. When he stepped out his white shorts were crimson.

Gordon has told me that Gregory loved to communicate by mail and even a short note—a hastily scribbled "Teach me the Double Haul"—would prompt a six- or seven-page missive in return, the pages thick with diagrams. That's how Gordon learned the Double Haul. (Not the ideal way, of course; the ideal way is to have an Old Guy stand beside you, exhorting you to haul with vigour and conviction.)

I guess that by this point in my little book, fishing has become a kind of metaphor. Granted, it has become that chiefly because no damn fish are being caught, but let's let it play out on that level for a little while. The wonderful thing here is that knowledge is being passed on from Old Guy to younger, for no other reason than the fact that knowledge was sought. Too many fields of human endeavour have become academies, in a most archaic sense; the questor after wisdom has first to display talent and worth. Gordon never demanded talent—I myself have next to none, and yet quickly became one of his protégés—and asked only that one be a reasonable person and act with a bit of human decency.

For some reason, I stood upon my rock and cast as well as I ever have. A large rock lay perhaps eighty feet away, and I propelled my Despair towards it effortlessly, landing the fly just beyond and slightly upriver, so that the water's sweep would pull it lazily through the slower dark water that clung to the boulder.

A strange intrusive reflection here, but it ties in, I'm sure, because *reflecting* is what one does when casting into a river.

Gordon has a unique way of affixing the leader to the fly line. No nail knots for Gordon. He shaves the end of the thick line, angles it like a carrot in a fancy French restaurant, so that when doubled back it forms a loop and the conjoining is unobtrusive. This is bound with a neat and linear row of thread, which is later lacquered for added strength. Gordon devised a clever system for winding the thread quickly and tightly, designing a heavy metal sheath for the thread bobbin. This is then set into orbit around the line. You use your thumbs to direct the thread, keeping it uniform and tight. If none of this makes any sense, don't worry about it, because it's not all that important. What's important is that it requires a certain skill to work the weighted bobbin correctly. So hitherto, whenever I bought a new fly line, I took it over to Gordon's and bade him help me.

One day, not so very long ago, I acquired a new fly line. I acquired it for a very specific reason. A few days earlier the editor of a prestigious magazine had telephoned me and asked, "How'd you like to stay in one of the fine old lodges on Vancouver Island and fish for steelhead for a week?" He then told me how much he'd pay me to do this and waited patiently for a reply. He heard nothing from my end except a distant, high-pitched yawping. "Paul? What do you say? Yes or no?"

"I'm going to say *yes*," I replied, "just as soon as I'm done giggling."

Not wanting to fail miserably at my assignment, I went down to Skinner's and bought a new fly line, a special thing designed for steelheading. The last few feet have powdered tungsten mixed into the line, causing it to plummet to the bottom in the fast British Columbia rivers. (The tungsten, I was to learn, would also cause the line to cast with all the precision of a snapped telephone wire, sending my guide scurrying for cover.) Just prior to the trip, as I made my final preparations, I realized that I had a problem. Namely, I didn't know how I was going to affix the leader to the fly line. I still didn't know how to tie a nail knot. I'd only learned enough to know that I actually required a nail—and I didn't even have one. What I really needed to do, I told myself, was to go over to Gordon's and get him to work the lead-leader gizmo for me.

But I hadn't spoken to Gordon for a couple of years. A couple of reasonably peaceful years. It was kind of a relief, not having Gordon talking me into doing things that I'd just as soon not do. Still, the lead-leader gizmo was the best method I knew of ...

I picked up the phone, punched in Gordon's number. I will never forget that telephone number. It has a pleasing symmetry and the numbers obligingly fall into any number of mnemonic systems, but that's not the reason I remember it so well.

He answered, typically, before it was through the first ring. "Yo?"

"Gordon?"

"Yes, sir."

"It's Paul. Kew."

"Yes, sir! What can I do for you?"

"Well, I've got a new fly line, you see, and I'd like you to help me fix it up."

"Oh." Gordon allowed a touch of annoyance to creep into that single syllable. I was more or less expecting it.

"I guess you don't really want to, huh?"

"You can come over and I'll help you one more time," he said.

"I see."

"The thing is, Kew—"

"Uh-huh?"

"I can't keep helping you do it, or you'll never be able to help someone *else* do it."

Not only did I still have an Old Guy, I myself was now an *apprentice* Old Guy. I could almost feel my paunch distending and curly white hairs shooting out of my ears. Still, the revelation made me very happy.

And when I returned from the Vancouver Island trip, I immediately telephoned Gordon.

"How did you make out?" he asked.

"Not so good with the fly line," I replied. I'd taken fish on the West Coast gear, strong rods with big metal level-wind reels attached. "The river was too damn fast."

"Why didn't you do an S-cast?"

"An S-cast?"

"Yeah. Throw a lot of curves into the line, so by the time it's straightened out, it's already sunk."

"Um ... did you teach me that one?"

"I must have taught you that."

"So," I asked quietly, "do you want to go fishing?"

We fished a day in early spring, and we fished in fine style, motoring across southern Ontario in his big land-boat, driving carelessly across farmers' fields. We snuck through people's backyards and ignored the barking of their guard dogs. The guard dogs too often gave themselves away, wagging the tips of their tails, sometimes almost imperceptibly but enough to let us know that when we dropped onto their side of the fence the beasts would stop barking and give us directions to the river. We fished for steelhead, anadromous rainbow trout. Gordon took a large one from a small pool on someone's private property, fighting the fish in complete silence because many times he'd been thrown off that same private property.

We worked our way upriver, and we found the honeymoon hotel for fish. The river fanned out and slowed down, and there we saw rainbow trout, scores and scores of them, each pair attending to the digging of the redd, one standing guard, the other digging out the bottom with a furious twisting motion. My Old Guy and I cast a few times, but the fish were no more interested in eating than you or I would be were we in the act of turning down the covers with our true love by our side. (Actually, I might want a small snack, but I've sacrificed candour for poetry here, a good deal every time.)

I suppose there might have been a way to catch those fish. Some specific fly, some combination of colour and motion that would make them strike out angrily. If Gordon knew it, he never mentioned it. He laid down his rod and fanned his arms towards the water, speechless in the presence of all the finny life.

And upon my rock back on Murphy's Island, I continued to cast. I aimed for the seams of water that lay behind and between rocks, where flows of disparate speed melded. I aimed for dark water and shadows. I threw the Despair across the river, hauling with vigour and conviction.

I caught nothing.

So now is as good a time as any to wonder, *where were all the fish?*

It's not as though my companions and I didn't spend an awful lot of time theorizing. Was it possible, we wondered, that a falls of some great height lay upriver, that coming to us would have meant almost certain death for fish? According to the map, the world was stitched together by elevation marks. These could indicate a drop of five feet or a drop of a hundred. Another theory had to do with the shallowness, the rockiness, the general uninvitingness of Q Lake. Or was our little island home to huge predatory pike? I'd seen one, had it irritably smash the little Mepps off my line. Trout and pike can coexist, of course, but maybe Murphy's Isle was a club hangout. Maybe nothing but thirty-pound pike lurked. In which case, you're thinking, we would have caught some. Good point. None of these theories have the resonance of correctness, do they?

I've no doubt that there are readers out there who know where to find fault: with the anglers. *I can't believe these guys,* they tell their husbands or wives with a smirk. *Despairs don't work in northern Quebec.* Or perhaps we'd trampled the bank furze too loudly, sending the specks off with silent eeks and shrieks. Or spooked the fish with too much false-casting.

Gordon remembers fishing the Broadback the first time, all those years ago. He stood by the water and waved his wand over and over again, carefully aiming for the dark water. Their guide, Maxim, came up behind Gordon, stilled his arm. "Too much," he said, waving his arm in the air. "Scare fish."

These are the same speckled trout from that rearing experiment, remember, the little Assinica fishies hiding from the scientists that they knew were bringing them food. This is why the Double Haul is so important, because there is only one laying out of line before shooting. And it can be made away from the target, the thin shadow darting across the water downriver. Now myself, I'd often cast two or three times, releasing in succession the loops in my left hand so that they didn't all bunch up in the first guide, so it's quite possible that I was spooking fish. But, hell, I'm not such a bad caster that I spooked all the fish in the general vicinity. And Gordon took Maxim's advice to heart, certainly, one false cast and then the line would fly to another part of the river. So why wasn't Gordon catching fish?

I can't avoid speculation along these lines: something has screwed up the fishing. Now, our gap-toothed nimrod grandfathers, by and large, never went to northern Quebec to slaughter fish, so we can't lay blame on their doorstep. But Hydro-Québec had moved onto the land, and even though there was no real evidence of them, we knew they'd been there.

(The next day, while we paddled the canoe, Gordon said, "There's another tree they've marked."

("Hmm?"

("They're marking trees. I'm not sure why. Look up ahead, about two hundred yards. They've hung a little metal tag on a tree by the shoreline."

(I shaded my eyes and squinted. "I can't see it."

("It's almost exactly straight ahead."

("How big is this tag?"

("Oh," answered Gordon, "about the size of a quarter.")

It's not necessary, I don't think, to believe the tales of science fiction. Hydro-Québec probably hasn't turned any rivers around. For one thing, I don't see what they'd get out of the deal. But maybe they just wanted to prove they could. Or maybe there is some bitter genius whose parents were washed out into James Bay, and it is his evil illogic to reverse all rivers so that parents are deposited safely back at the headwaters. It's a possibility, sure. (Humour me.) And although our area looked virgin and untouched, we had no idea what havoc Hydro-Québec was wreaking up- or downriver. From the air, we'd only seen two endless roads cut through the wilderness, straight and true. But there might be other areas where the devastation was more obvious, where the land was now as lifeless as the moon. It's kind of easy, not to mention fun, to indulge these theories of bureaucratic malfeasance. For example, one day a government helicopter came and hovered over our campsite. Were they making sure we were all right—*or making sure we hadn't learned too much?* But more likely is the thought that the simple presence of humans in number—even if gentle and conscientious—had screwed up everything.

We are not the only anglers who have fared badly in the northern extreme. On the way in, we'd met four fishermen from Ohio on their way out. They were filthy and beard-stubbled, their eyes ringed from sleeplessness and too much beer. They'd been to the Rupert, even farther north than we'd camped. They had a cooler with one fish in it. Granted, it was a nice, big fish, but it was shockingly unaccompanied.

And allow me a moment to say, things is weird all over. I don't know what we've done, what giant clock spring we've wound too tight, but the fishing is pretty bad everywhere you go.

Although actually, I've chosen my words poorly. I should say what Gordon says—what he in fact said when we flew out of the bush, his answer to the fat man with the little poodle who drove a brand-new Cadillac and seemed to have nothing better to do than hang around a tiny airport.

"How was the fishing?" the fat man asked.

"The fishing was excellent, sir," responded my Old Guy. "The *catching* left something to be desired."

Paulo and I hurried back to camp, intending to cook a fine meal to welcome the fellows. We didn't manage that, of course, although we did put on the kettle and were able to offer Gary and Gordon well-steeped if chilly cups of tea upon their return.

Gordon was clearly exhausted from the paddle, but he was almost deliriously happy. The Falls downriver—only five miles, he and Gary thought—were beautiful. More to the point, although they hadn't had long to angle there, Gary had taken a fish.

"Great!" shouted Paulo and I, half because it meant that we might have the chance to catch one, half because we knew we would definitely get the chance to eat one.

Gordon immediately began cooking. "'Oh, yes,'" he sang, "'I'm the great believer...'"

"That's not right," I put in. I hadn't been meaning to speak; I just am, upon occasion, a hopeless pedant.

"Hmmm?"

"It's not 'great believer,' it's 'great pretender.'"

"Is it? Hmmmm..."

But that was churlish of me, because my Old Guy *is* the great believer.

We climbed into the canoe, that next day, that beautiful next day that broke cloudless, Murphy-less.

The evening before, after eating Gary's fish, we had sat around and belched while Gary strummed his guitar, playing a tune he'd composed on an earlier trip to the Broadback. Gordon started requesting songs and remarked that a number of them had, for titles, the names of women. So we began playing that game in which you go through the alphabet, each taking a turn naming a song with a woman's name. We played this game as we climbed into our sleeping bags. I could not think of the name of a certain instrumental by the Allman Brothers. (I still can't.) Gary started, suddenly, sitting bolt upright on his cot and saying, "Uh oh! I have to go to the bog." He stumbled out of the tent into the blackness.

"I've got one!" said Gordon.

"It's my turn," said I.

"*Alma May!*"

"It's my turn, and I'm on *J*."

From without came the most horrible sort of wailing, managing to be both heartbroken and inhuman at the same time.

Gordon, singing the song *Alma May* under his breath—not that I believe there is any such song—got to his feet, clutching his sleeping bag around him primly, and peered through the tent flap. "Hey, guys!" he said, delighted. "We got an abominable snowman out here."

Out in the furze, the abominable snowman was, basically, doing calisthenics, but I've decided to tell you that the creature was dancing, its muscles plucked and twitched by the moon. It continued its odd ululations, a hideous baying to the dark side.

I was not frightened at all. This was the first sign I'd had in many long days that there was life on the island—other than four mugs and a demented squirrel—even if it was only a middle-aged jazz musician in a white anticontamination suit. Gary had secreted the suit in his duffle for this exact occasion. Now here he was dancing about in his white suit, and though his face was obscured by silvery mesh, I knew he was grinning like an idiot. We all were.

And you know, the next morning there was a bird in the camp, a whiskey-jack. Gary smiled in its direction, adjusted his hat and climbed into the bow of the canoe. Paulo and I took up the midships, deciding upon respective sides and inclining our beef towards them. Gordon climbed into the stern of the War Canoe, and we headed off towards the Falls.

We fell into cadence, following Gary's lead. The canoe moved across Q Lake. A brace of skittish ducks squawked along in front of us, raising and setting their fannies every fifty feet or so.

"How big are the Falls?" I asked, ever the worrywart.

"Big," said Gary,

"Fairly big," corrected Gordon. "Paulo, you've gotten out of rhythm."

"But they're not dangerous?"

"I wouldn't want to go over them," said Gary.

"Look," said my Old Guy, "we'll *hear* them before we ever see them. As soon as we do, we put onto shore and go on by foot."

And the reason I've recorded that conversation is that it was entirely and perfectly true. Long before they showed themselves, the Falls announced their existence by filling the air with soggy hiss, sizzle and crack. And it seems to me there's a lesson to be learned. At least, I learned one. I could spell it out in a kind of homey philosophic manner, but, well, it's bad enough to have written a fishing book where precious few fish get caught without trying to make up for it with bucolic platitudes. So I will concentrate only on the effect.

That low-grade panic, the bad sweat I'd brought with me from the city, had suddenly and miraculously disappeared. And not just momentarily, either, I can report with hind-sight, because when the Otter took off the next day, I was the little kid sitting in the cockpit with the captain. Fear of flying is a handy little travelling bag in which to dump unfocussed terror, so it makes a good test case. And it was so far gone that one of my first acts upon regaining civilization—after kissing the appropriate people lustily—was to telephone a flight academy and make inquiries about ground school.

I had had no epiphany, no great revelation. I had merely seen, for the first time, a logic and its flawlessness.

I can give you an example of this logic. There at the Falls I caught a fallfish. It weighed about a pound and was covered with huge prehistoric scales, as though it had been waiting an eternity for me to catch it.

I released it back into the river—fine river, fine world— and continued fishing with my Old Guy.

$\mathcal{E}$ P I L O G U E

LAST NIGHT, I ATTENDED THE Scarborough Fly and Bait Casting Association's annual Christmas party. I admit, it was a function that I'd half a mind to duck, but I went for a couple of reasons.

One was to get my fishing rod from Paulo. You'll recall that I'd left half of it behind in the bush on Murphy's Island, so when we arrived back from Quebec, I had gone down into Gordon's basement and sorted through the mountain of junk there until I found a suitable rod tip, itself lost beside some river until reclaimed by Gordon. The piece was unfortunately cracked and splintered around the receiving end. Gordon was, of course, full of instruction, explaining how to wrap monofilament around the defect, but at some point he looked up into my eyes and saw that I was not taking this in. He patted the piece of fishing rod gently. "Maybe Paulo will do it for you," Gordon suggested.

Which is what Paulo had done, and he'd called to say that he would bring the rod to the annual Christmas party. So although it had been some time since I'd cast with the men and women of the Scarborough Fly and Bait Casting Association, I drove northward into the heart of Scarborough.

The party was not at Gordon's house, rather at a house a couple of blocks away. I was greeted by a young couple, Dave and Ella, who made me welcome as children of various ages scurried about behind them. The kids didn't all belong to Dave and Ella, mind you; most of the club members were now parents, it seemed. Although all were younger than I, there had been a quantum leap in the maturity of the membership. Still, there was a sameness about them, something recognizable and identifying. It wasn't anything so simple as a shared physicality, although stockiness was the order of the day, tournament casting being a bit like sumo wrestling in its conception of the perfect athlete. No, what I recognized was more ethereal than any of that. There was an attitude of affability, a great deal of locker-room banter and teasing in which everyone, men and women alike, took part. When someone would tell a fishing story, he or she was allowed the floor, and everyone would inch forward on the sofas or hunker down nearby. There was—not that it should have been such a great surprise—a sense of community. And I suppose that was what I had been looking for, ten years earlier, even more than casting skills or fishing acumen.

There was even a sense in which I was the prodigal son. Gordon sat in the middle of the party, looking hale but immobilized somewhat by a recent battle with a huge kidney stone. "Kew!" he yelled, surprised and delighted that I'd come to the party, even though he'd called almost daily for the past week to remind me about it. "Come here and sit down." He meant in the chair immediately beside his own. I took it, but Gordon did not speak to me immediately; instead he surveyed the room and grinned, finding it to be good. He patted my knee, intuiting my restlessness and keeping me still. And there we sat for many long moments. When he did speak, it was about his medical complaints. I listened dutifully, and left to get a soft drink at the first opportunity.

Paulo had—like myself—regained the weight he'd lost on the fishing trip. He stood in the kitchen grinning, his arms folded across his chest. I admired the work he'd done on my rod, which was now whole and complete again. The colours and wrappings were mismatched, but I sensed—and the summer to come would prove this—that it was now a better, more reliable stick. I don't think Nietzsche was thinking about fishing rods when he came up with "What does not destroy me, makes me stronger," but it's no less true.

Paulo had been working very hard in the four months since our return, taking a course that had improved his standing and status at work and, not coincidentally, given him a lot more responsibility and, uh, *work*. He'd not been regular in his club attendance, with the result that he'd lost his title as the club's best caster, a situation that he accepted with good grace and humour.

"Do you know what?" he asked me. "I love to listen to classical music now." I remembered how his eyes had lit up that evening when we were bathed in the aurora, when I'd affixed Beethoven's Seventh over his ears. On the long car ride home, he'd asked if he could hear it again, and he'd sat through the symphony with great concentration, in total serenity. "I listen to this music all the time," Paulo told me. "In the morning, afternoon and night. It's like an obsession."

Gary wasn't at the party, having a gig that night. He regularly sends me little flyers now, announcing when groups that he's part of are playing at Toronto's clubs.

But there was at that party a young man named Rick Matusiak, a quiet and diffident sort who had a remarkable story to tell. Gordon had mentioned this fellow to me once or twice. Matusiak is one of the most obsessed anglers who ever walked the face of the planet, and that is surely going some. Matusiak had, sometime the previous year, sought out Gordon, whose book *Fishin' Hats* Rick carried with him always as a kind of talisman. Matusiak had sent Gordon a video illustrating some of the things he was up to. For example, he was raising a pair of rainbow trout in a large apartment aquarium. He had recorded himself ice fishing, holding up a chunk of ice and showing how it had honeycombed, how the slightest pressure would cause its seeming solidity to explode away into nothingness. He had got this chunk of ice from *just where he was standing* at the time.

I joined a little crowd around Matusiak just as someone related a story of ice-fishing danger, a couple of frigid anglers suddenly separated from the shore by a rift of icy water. Matusiak nodded, citing this as quite common. "The thing to do," he noted calmly, "is to always have a portable spade. Make a boat out of some of the ice you're standing on. Paddle across to the mainland. It takes a few hours but at least you'll be dry. A lot of guys panic and try to swim it."

Now, back to that remarkable story Matusiak had to tell. I should point out, although the details are not known to me, that he'd been plagued the previous year with medical problems. I seem to recall Gordon saying something about a heart attack, but this could well be misremembered. Matusiak was not that old, somewhere in his thirties, and seemed healthy enough, if perhaps a bit high-strung. (He had telephoned Gordon earlier that day, wanting to know what people were wearing to the Christmas party. This is a little akin to wanting to know which plays of Shakespeare might be discussed at a ΔΠΔ keg bash.) He was shy, casting his gaze mostly downwards. Matusiak seemed to know few of the people there, although they all knew who he was.

Because there he had been, you see, sitting in his living room watching television, when his cousin suggested that they go fishing. There was perhaps an hour of daylight left, not much time to go adventuring. Matusiak lives to the east of the city of Toronto, where many fine rivers romp up from the grey lake. He thought initially about hightailing it over to one of these, perhaps the Ganaraska. Then he decided to simply head down to Lake Ontario, to cast from the shore near the hydro station. "It is a place," he told us quietly, "where I'd caught large fish before."

He fired a Little Cleo into the roiling water and almost immediately began to grapple with a large fish. "I was certain I had a big salmon on there," he related at the Christmas party, as members of the Scarborough Fly and Bait Casting Association pressed in upon him. "It took about half an hour to land it. Then I looked at it and I said, 'Hey, that's no salmon. That's a brown trout.'"

As Matusiak's luck would have it, there was a gentleman from the Ministry of Natural Resources not fifty feet away. He came over and looked at the fish. "I think we'd better get that weighed," he said.

Matusiak's fish bested the previous Ontario record by a good two pounds. It is also a world line-class record, although at the point in time when I'm actually typing this sentence, which exact record remains to be seen. The International Game Fish Association, the keepers of such arcana, demanded thirty feet of Matusiak's line to be tested, and the procedure was scheduled to take five months. Apparently the manufacturer's specifications are next to useless. Line labelled eight-pound test is as likely to be nearer six or ten.

The International Game Fish Association was founded in 1939 and became *the* body of record when the magazine *Field & Stream*—which had been recording fresh-water catches for sixty-eight years—turned over its historical data. Ernest Hemingway served as a vice-president from 1940 until his death in 1962. The IGFA publishes a book called *World Record Game Fishes*, and the next edition will include Rick Matusiak's name.

Later that same month Matusiak took a twenty-one-pound rainbow out of the Ganny. "I don't catch many fish," he told me, "but they tend to be large." His reputation in angling circles soaring, Rick had recently been approached by a magazine to write about his brown trout. He was, at the Christmas party, brimming with scientifical data culled from the library. "Large fish like that are either eunuchs or triploids," he told the gathering, who tilted their heads politely. "Either no sexual organs," he continued dryly, "or an extra set of chromosomes." One assumes this sort of mutation has to do with the poisoning of the Great Lake; it's hard to discount as coincidence the fact that Matusiak was fishing near a nuclear plant. One worries—*I* worry, damn it, this is no time for circumspection—about a world where one catches either nothing or overgrown neon monsters, many-eyed and multi-finned. "Eunuchs and triploids," Matusiak repeated, himself wary of the words, his face wrinkled with distaste. He was actually worried about the nature of the article he was writing. He was so obsessed with the scientific research he was doing that he feared the finished product would be unreadable.

Being a professional writer, I gave him what I considered sage advice. "Myself," I told him, "I don't do *any* research. That way I don't get bogged down in all the details."

"Uh-huh."

"Did you have any sense, when you left for the lake, that something was about to happen?"

Matusiak shrugged. He has a fairly extensive repertoire of shrugs, this one seeming to mean that he knew more than he was saying. "Oh, you know," he began hesitantly. "I had a feeling that something was going to happen."

"Really?"

He shrugged once more. "I suppose, in my mind, I'd caught that fish a thousand times. I'd been through it over and over again."

"At the same place?"

"Yes."

"You knew it was going to happen?"

"It's a place," Matusiak repeated, "where I've caught big fish before."

"I go up north to this place, Wolverine Lodge," I told him. Journalistically speaking, I was trying to put Rick at his ease. Mind you, the volume and pitch of my voice were unprofessionally raised. "And there's this place, by the second set of narrows, where there's a big stone face before the river widens out, you know, and I've *seen* myself catch a *huge* pike there. I even forget when I saw it, how long ago or in waking dream or slumber. But once or twice a year I'll go out on the vision quest, you know, I'll get out the pike stick and go and cast something big off the cliff face. And I never catch anything, but it doesn't matter. One day I will."

Matusiak shrugged but nodded gently. "That's not the sort of thing," he pointed out, "that people like to read."

I imagine that Gordon has had a vision of himself catching a magnificent speckled trout, working it out of the furious dark water of the Broadback watershed. Perhaps a fisherman holds visions even more dear than memories.

The day after our return from Murphy's Island, Gordon started firing off letters to the Quebec government. In effect they read, "Thank you very much, but I have to go back once again. You didn't allow me to get to my spot, the Old Place I love most in my heart, and that is where it must and will happen." We have yet to hear back. I don't know how likely it is that any more expeditions will be mounted. Paulo might return, although I don't think so. He was disappointed, and a young man's disappointment is obdurate. Gary has announced, with finality and certainty, that he won't go back, although the day of the canoe trip to the Falls he did half-bake a scheme to trip through an extreme river or two.

As for myself, I would have to rate the odds as low. There are simply too many places left to fish. I was deeply affected by a brief conversation with Charles Gaines, author and angler. "Where on the globe," I asked him, "haven't you fished?"

"I've heard there's good fishing in Nepal," he replied, "and there are some rivers in Russia I must get to."

That is the sort of answer I would like to give, although I doubt that I'll even make all the continents.

But something within me is drawn back to the extreme, like Gordon, even though its beauty is so austere that many would fail to recognize it as beauty at all. It is unvariated and seemingly endless. It can be brutal. But it is a place where you can see the hand of God, even if He has only torn out a blank page from His notebook and let it flutter to land on top of the world. It is a place where a little man can leave a big mark.

But my conversation with Rick Matusiak reminded me of something, and I took my place again beside Gordon.

"I checked the IGFA record book," I said.

"Hm-mmm?"

"That fish you took thirty years ago, when you went in with your buddy and Maxim Moisim, the eleven-pounder?"

"Yes?"

"That's the largest speckled trout ever taken on a fly. The one the IGFA has listed is ten pounds, seven ounces. You have the world record."

Gordon smiled slightly, and shrugged.

About the Author

Paul Quarrington was born in Toronto in 1953. His 1987 novel, *King Leary*, won the Stephen Leacock Medal for Humor, and *Whale Music*, published in 1989, was given the Governor General's Award, Canada's top book prize. A longtime and dedicated member of the Scarborough Fly and Bait Casting Association, he is no stranger to writing about the denizens of the deep. His novel, *The Life of Hope*, featured a 2000-year-old fish named Ol' Mossback.